I0818893

THE ART *TRAVEL* BOOK

40 iconic outdoor artworks

Nadine van den Bosch
Nienke van der Wal

Europe

The Americas

Introduction

From the time of the earliest cave paintings to the present day, nature has always been a source of inspiration for artists. Over the centuries, nature has featured in art as backdrop, muse, symbol and subject. In the 1960s, a shift occurred: nature was no longer just a topic – it became the canvas and even the material itself. From the American desert to the vineyards in France, from the forests of Thailand to the Japanese coastline, artworks began to emerge that were inseparable from the places where they were made.
Those projects, featured in this book, stand on the shoulders of earlier traditions and connect back to artists who, long before, were already inspired by the sky, the land or the sea. Before we encourage you to head outdoors in the next chapters, we invite you on a short journey through art history to see where this fascination with nature began, and how it evolved across the centuries.

Art and Nature Through the Ages
Indigenous peoples have long created artworks tied to the landscape, predating western land art by millennia. About 40,000 to 60,000 years ago, Aboriginal artists in Australia made ceremonial rock arrangements, songlines and ground paintings. Around the same time, the oldest known cave paintings – depictions of animals – were created in Leang Tedongnge, Indonesia. As human societies developed during the Bronze Age, artists across the Mediterranean began to celebrate the natural world in their work. On the island of Santorini, for instance, the vibrant frescoes of Akrotiri show swallows and flowering branches. Similar natural motifs appeared in Minoan Crete and ancient Egypt, and later in ancient Rome, roughly 2,000 years ago. In India, art from this period often reflected a deep spiritual connection to the natural world: the murals of the Ajanta Caves that were created about 1,500 years ago, for example, depict forests, rivers and animals as part of sacred narratives. And in the Islamic world, around 10 to 12 centuries ago, nature was transformed into pattern and geometry, with gardens and mosaics evoking paradise on earth. Across medieval Europe, vines, flowers and animals decorated sacred texts and cathedrals, while in the same period in East Asia, artists such as Guo Xi rendered mountains and landscapes not merely as scenery but as expressions of harmony, transience and reflection.

Though, as shown above, art and nature have long been intertwined across cultures, art history has mostly been told from a western perspective. It is important to note that European movements like Baroque, Romanticism and Impressionism – all movements that are linked to nature and which we will delve into next – represent only one narrative thread. In Asia, Africa, Oceania and the Americas, art evolved through different structures – both through different traditions of ritual and spirituality, and through colonial encounter or postcolonial expression. We will also see how European art was influenced by colonial encounters as much as the other way around. In the end, all these artists from all over the world have one thing in common: the shared desire to represent, honour or collaborate with nature.

Jacob van Ruisdael, Landscape with a Village in the Distance

Baroque
In the Netherlands in the 17th century, landscape painting emerged as an independent genre, flourishing in a growing art market that catered to the rising middle class. The Netherlands had no towering mountains or wild forests, yet painters turned their attention to the everyday surroundings that defined the country: rivers, dunes and farmland. What might have seemed ordinary became extraordinary on canvas. These works offered viewers a vision of their homeland as both familiar and elevated – calm at times, powerful or ominous at others.

Artists such as Jacob van Ruisdael and Jan van Goyen shaped this tradition. They mastered the art of composition, using low horizons to stretch the sky across most of the painting. Clouds and light weren't just background details – they became the main characters, shaping mood and atmosphere. Those vast, shifting Dutch skies remain instantly recognisable today. Take Jacob van Ruisdael's *Landscape with a Village in the Distance*. Built from the essentials – earth, water and air – the scene feels monumental despite its modest subject matter. The heavy cumulus clouds overhead bring a sense of drama, reminding us how much power lies in the sky above the flat land.

Even Rembrandt van Rijn, best known for his portraits, turned to the natural world for inspiration. In *Landscape with a Stone Bridge*, he painted a landscape that never actually existed. Stone bridges of this kind were found only in cities at the time, so this countryside view is clearly a product of his imagination. The painting may be small, but it feels lively and atmospheric: dark clouds gather while a ray of sunlight breaks through. Rembrandt worked indoors, freely adjusting light and colour – much as we now use filters to manipulate the photos we take with our phones – to create mood in his paintings rather than a literal record of a scene.

Baroque was brought to South America by Spanish and Portuguese colonisers and reinterpreted locally in churches and mission art. In places like Mexico, Peru and Brazil, Indigenous artists blended Baroque with native flora, fauna and symbols (often referred to as Mestizo Baroque). Countries in Asia, specifically the Philippines (then under Spanish rule), also developed a tropical Baroque with local materials and coastal motifs.

Romanticism

By the late 18th century, a new movement swept across Europe. Romanticism broke with the cool logic and order of the Enlightenment, placing emotion, imagination and the individual at the centre of artistic expression. It was a time of upheaval: the French Revolution challenged old systems of power, while the Industrial Revolution transformed cities and landscapes. Against this backdrop, artists turned to nature as both escape and inspiration. For painters, the landscape became a stage for human emotions. Caspar David Friedrich, one of the great artists of the era, created works in which nature seemed to echo the inner life of the viewer. His famous image of a lone figure on a rocky peak, gazing out across a sea of fog, captures both the vastness of the world and the solitude of human existence. We see the figure only from the back, leaving their identity unknown and placing even greater emphasis on nature as the main character of this painting.

In Britain, J.M.W. Turner took a different approach but shared the same fascination with the sublime. He painted storms, mountains and oceans not as passive scenes, but as overwhelming forces. In *Snow Storm – Steam-Boat off a Harbour's Mouth*, Turner is said to have drawn on his own harrowing experience of being caught in violent weather at sea, after allegedly having tied himself to a ship's mast to feel the full force of nature first-hand. His whirling brushstrokes and turbulent light don't just show us nature's power – they throw us into it. In Asia, particularly Japan, ukiyo-e (woodblock) prints by artists like Hokusai and Hiroshige captured landscapes and the power of natural forces – waves, storms, mountains – that resonate strongly with Romantic ideals of the sublime. The same can be said for Latin American artists such as the Mexican artist José María Velasco, who painted sweeping views of valleys and volcanoes.

Caspar David Friedrich, Wanderer above the Sea of Fog

冨嶽三十六景
神奈川沖
浪裏

Hokusai, The Great Wave off Kanagawa

Guo Xi, Early Spring

Impressionism

In the mid-19th century, a group of French painters began to break away from academic tradition. Instead of depicting carefully staged historical or mythological scenes, they set out to capture the world as it unfolded before their eyes. What mattered was the immediate impression of a moment: the shimmer of light on water, the haze of morning fog and the quick shift of clouds. Their approach was radical: loose brushwork, bright colours and a focus on atmosphere rather than detail. Thanks to the recent invention of paint in portable tubes, artists could leave their studios and work outdoors. Painting *en plein air* allowed them to chase the changing effects of light directly on canvas.

Claude Monet's *Impression, Sunrise* gave the movement its name. With just a few strokes of colour, the painting suggests both the calm of a harbour at dawn and the fleeting sensation of seeing it in real time. Monet, Pierre-Auguste Renoir and their peers weren't just painting landscapes; they were painting experience itself. Building on the innovations of the Impressionists, Vincent van Gogh carried the connection between art and nature into new territory. For him, landscapes weren't simply scenes to be observed; they also became expressions of raw emotion. His fields ripple with movement, his cypress trees twist upwards with intensity and his night skies seem alive with swirling light. Van Gogh's paintings don't just record what nature looks like; they communicate what it feels like to stand within it.

Impressionists and Post-Impressionists such as van Gogh and Édouard Manet were heavily influenced by Japanese art, most famously reflected in van Gogh's *Almond Blossom*. In turn, Japanese painters began combining western techniques with traditional aesthetics. Meanwhile in India, under British colonial rule, the Bengal School of Art arose, blending local spirituality and natural imagery with Impressionist techniques. Latin American Impressionism developed in cities like Buenos Aires (Argentina), Montevideo (Uruguay) and Mexico City (Mexico), where artists such as Armando Reverón (Venezuela) and Andrés de Santa María (Colombia) explored light and atmosphere in ways parallel to, yet distinct from, their European counterparts.

Land Art

By the mid-20th century, artists began to look beyond canvases and gallery walls. The landscape itself became their medium. Out of this shift came the Land Art movement of the 1960s and '70s that saw artists building works on a scale that only deserts, lakes or open fields could hold. These weren't sculptures that could be relocated or displayed indoors. They were inseparable from the earth around them and became a permanent part of nature itself. The roots of the Land Art movement lie in a turbulent moment in history.

The Vietnam War, environmental awareness and the first photographs of Earth seen from space all contributed to a new perspective. Artists questioned power structures, resisted the commercialisation of art and looked for ways to make their work more open, public and democratic.

American artists like Robert Smithson, Nancy Holt, Walter De Maria and Michael Heizer rejected the white cube of the museum, turning instead to the vast American landscape as their canvas. What united these projects was their accessibility: many land artworks were, and still are, free for anyone to visit. Land art expanded rapidly, soon spreading worldwide, and adapted to local landscapes and histories. Working with living matter rather than paint also demanded a very different process from artists, one that often blurred the line between creation and collaboration with nature. At the same time, many projects reflected humanity's enduring tendency to shape and control the natural world, even while seeking to honour it.

Art in Nature

While all land art exists in a natural environment, not all outdoor art is land art. In this book we share some well-known land art, such as the works of Walter De Maria and Maya Lin, but we also highlight other kinds of art in nature. Some are public artworks, free to visit – such as our cover piece, *Seven Magic Mountains* by Ugo Rondinone in the Nevada desert, Jenny Holzer's works in the Swiss mountains or Yoko Ono's tower on an Icelandic island. Others are part of museums or cultural sites, such as Louise Bourgeois's sculpture in a traditional garden in South Korea, Jeppe Hein's installation on the French island of Porquerolles or James Turrell's light installation in the Argentinian mountains.

As you may have noticed when first opening this book, many of these works are located in the West: Europe and North America. That is no coincidence. Although we have tried to bring in as much variety as possible in terms of geography, as well as artists' background, gender, age, artistic approach and medium, many of the best-known works still come from a familiar group: mostly male, mostly western – the usual suspects. This raises important questions: whose vision of nature are we seeing? Whose voices are absent? This book aims to broaden the perspective – to introduce new names alongside the established ones and to highlight how art in the open can, and should, become more inclusive.

Public art often appears democratic – outdoors, free, available to all. But in reality, the highest concentration of works remains in wealthier regions of the world. So who actually gets to see these pieces? These are questions not only about art, but about the privilege of travel itself. In this guide, we try to strike a balance between celebrating both iconic works and overlooked ones, while including diverse artists and contexts, and showing how art and nature continue to shape one another. This book is also an invitation – a call to action for decision makers – to diversify our beloved natural and artistic landscape even further.

Lastly
Whether you use this book to dream or to create an itinerary for a trip around the globe, we hope the artworks serve as a window to another way of seeing, thinking and experiencing the world. And if you do go for a visit, please know you will find practical details via the links behind the QR codes.

We wish you happy travels!
Nadine van den Bosch & Nienke van der Wal

Europe

01.

Alicja Kwade
Pars pro Toto

Louisiana Museum of Modern Art, Humlebæk, Denmark

The Latin phrase 'pars pro toto' translates to 'a part for the whole' – referring to the idea that a portion of an object, place or concept is used to represent its entirety. And that is exactly what Alicja Kwade does here: she shows us eight enormous stones, reminiscent of planets, and in doing so, effortlessly leads us to contemplate the vast planetary system – the universe – that we are a tiny part of. As you stand looking at this installation, you yourself are, in fact, standing on a sphere much like the ones you are observing, all the while spinning through space at a bewildering speed. With this work, Kwade points out the absurdity of our existence: the universe's endless time and immense scale make our presence here feel random. It is quite poetic how stones of such modest size can so poignantly remind us of our own smallness.

At the same time, Kwade also brings the world to our feet – literally. The orbs are carved out of stone – marble, granite, quartzite– quarried in different parts of the world. Under Kwade's direction, each stone was carefully shaped into a perfect sphere by German stonemasons, maintaining the natural veins and layers within the rock, showing traces of geological processes that span millions of years. The concentric patterns of the smooth spheres resemble planetary surfaces, as seen from afar.

The work is connected to similar pieces by Kwade in other parts of the world. You can find other examples in the Kalasatama neighbourhood of Helsinki (Finland), on the campus of Stanford University in California, and on the Ann & Monroe Carell Jr. Family Sculpture Trail at Cheekwood garden in Nashville, Tennessee (USA) – the latter alongside sculptures by James Turrell (p. 142), Jenny Holzer (p. 48) and Jaume Plensa. Kwade's work *LinienLand*, featuring large stones precariously balanced and seemingly floating within a metal grid at Storm King Art Center (New Windsor, USA), was conceived during her work on *Pars pro Toto*.

ABOUT ALICJA KWADE

Alicja Kwade was born in 1979 in Katowice, Poland. Kwade uses sculpture and installations to explore how we understand time, space and the material world, posing philosophical questions and inviting viewers to see reality from a shifted perspective. Her work reflects on the absurdity of our existence as much as it questions the world around us and the constructs we have created.

'I attempt to acknowledge nothingness as real. If nothing is real, there are only possibilities.'

Alicja Kwade

Other things to do in and around the Louisiana Museum of Modern Art

- **LOUISIANA MUSEUM SCULPTURE PARK**

  There are many other artworks to visit in the Louisiana Museum's sculpture garden, including works by Henry Moore, Alexander Calder and Joan Miró.

- **COPENHAGEN PUBLIC ART**

  The Danish capital Copenhagen is a great city for art lovers. Independent galleries and artist-run spaces thrive in neighbourhoods like Vesterbro and Nørrebro, while public art by Copenhagen-born artists Olafur Eliasson (p. 80) and Jeppe Hein (p. 52) can be found in the city centre.

- **ARKEN MUSEUM & SCULPTURE GARDEN**

  Just below the city of Copenhagen, you will find the ARKEN Museum of Contemporary Art, with a sculpture garden of its own focusing on contemporary Danish and Nordic artists. The museum's architecture, resembling a boat or ark, blends in beautifully with the Danish coast.

ARKEN Museum of Contemporary Art

02.

Anselm Kiefer
La Ribaute

Eschaton — Anselm Kiefer Foundation, Barjac, France

On the outskirts of Barjac in southern France, Anselm Kiefer has created *La Ribaute*, a massive artwork built on the grounds of a former silk factory. The site, managed by the Eschaton Foundation (named after a term meaning 'the end of time'), spans over 40 hectares and includes more than 60 buildings, underground tunnels, towers, glasshouses and vast installation halls. This is not a museum or a sculpture park, but an entire environment shaped by Kiefer's exploration of history, memory and time.

As a visitor, you are not simply walking through an exhibition but entering a place that feels like a memory made physical. Some parts are open to the sky; others are hidden below ground. You descend narrow staircases into concrete corridors, lit only by small skylights or dim bulbs. Underground spaces resemble bunkers, tombs or abandoned archives. These spaces are not just architectural; they reinforce Kiefer's interest in the layering and burying of meaning.

Kiefer uses materials like lead, ash, straw, clay and concrete – not for their beauty, but for their symbolism. Lead, for example, is linked to knowledge in alchemy. While it is heavy and difficult to work with, it is also enduring. Straw and ash together reference life and destruction. These materials allow Kiefer to address themes such as post-war trauma, the erasure and rewriting of history, and the cyclical nature of decay and rebirth.

Throughout the site, recurring motifs appear: books made of lead, scorched sunflowers, towers built from concrete blocks. In glasshouses, you encounter a group of sculptures of headless female forms, modelled from dresses. These figures represent women from antiquity or mythology, whose stories have often been silenced or forgotten. Visits to this site are upon reservation through the website only.

die Frauen der Antike

ABOUT ANSELM KIEFER

Anselm Kiefer was born in 1945 in Donaueschingen, Germany. He is known for his monumental installations and paintings that explore history, mythology and memory. Kiefer is deeply influenced by post-war Germany, literature and Jewish mysticism. His artistic signature lies in the physicality of his work (layered, weathered and often monumental), creating spaces that confront the weight of the past while suggesting the possibility of transformation.

Three tips for art in nearby Arles

- **VAN GOGH WALK**
  Follow in the footsteps of Vincent van Gogh through Arles, where he painted some of his most iconic works. Several outdoor panels mark the exact locations depicted in his paintings, offering a self-guided tour through the artist's Provençal period. Interested in more van Gogh? Visit the Fondation Vincent van Gogh Arles, dedicated to the artist's life and work in the region.

- **LUMA ARLES**
  Located in a striking tower designed by architect Frank Gehry, LUMA Arles is a cultural complex combining contemporary art, photography, research and ecology. Inside, you'll find exhibitions by international artists, while the surrounding Parc des Ateliers features installations and landscaped gardens.

- **RENCONTRES D'ARLES**
  Held every summer since 1970, Rencontres d'Arles is one of the most important photography festivals in the world. Spread across historic venues in the city, the festival showcases a mix of emerging talents and major names in contemporary photography.

LUMA Arles

03.

Daniel Buren
A Sulle Vigne: punti di vista

Castello di Ama, Ama, Italy

In the rolling hills of Tuscany lies the Castello di Ama estate, where wine, art and nature come together. Scattered across the grounds are over 15 impressive artworks created specifically for this location. After a short walk descending among the picturesque stone buildings, you soon come face to face with one of the most iconic works from the collection: *Sulle Vigne: punti di vista (Among the vineyards: points of view)* by Daniel Buren.

The artist designed a 25-metre-long and 2-metre-high mirrored wall for Castello di Ama, interrupted by five large square openings that function as windows onto the landscape beyond. This imposing work is one of the most dynamic installations among the vineyards; by using mirrors, the installation constantly changes its appearance and fragments the landscape. Buren plays with the viewer's gaze: you see yourself reflected in the mirrored surface of the work, while at the same time the grapevines, landscape and sky appear in the five openings.

In the frames of the square cut-outs, you can see Buren's signature motif: perfectly straight stripes exactly 8.7 centimetres wide, rendered in black and white. Buren's artwork blends into its surroundings while also framing the landscape. As it does so, a wall suddenly becomes a window onto the world around us, instead of a barrier that blocks access.

ABOUT DANIEL BUREN

Daniel Buren was born in 1938 in Boulogne-Billancourt, France. He is a conceptual artist famed for his site-specific works and signature 8.7-centimetres-wide stripes in bold contrasting colours. Central to his work is his concern with the relationship between art and its surroundings, which he explores by integrating reflective surfaces and his signature stripe motif into public spaces. Buren's engaging interventions in both nature and the urban environment invite viewers to perceive environment, perspective and context anew.

'Even in rural areas, one sees fields, vineyards, and groves meticulously arranged by human labor. These traces of humanity provide a context for art to enter into dialogue.'

Daniel Buren

Other things to see at Castello di Ama

- **RONI HORN, Untitled**
  In a small, dimly lit room in Villa Ricucci, you will find a glass sculpture by Roni Horn. A round, solid-glass sculpture rests on the damp floor, its pale blue colour shifting with the changing natural light. The smooth surface and perfect circular shape remind us of a hard-boiled sweet, giving the work an inviting, almost edible allure.

- **HIROSHI SUGIMOTO, Confession of Zero**
  Hidden in an 18th-century chapel stands a monumental steel sculpture by Hiroshi Sugimoto. Its hidden spot rewards the determined art lover: the artwork can be found in the curved passage behind the altar. Installed within the historic space, *Confession of Zero* consists of two parts, based on a precise mathematical model – a lower half grounded below and an upper piece suspended above – creating a quiet, tense balance that heightens the chapel's contemplative atmosphere.

- **CARLOS GARAICOA, Yo no quiero ver más a mis vecinos**
  Carlos Garaicoa's *Yo no quiero ver más a mis vecinos (I don't want to see my neighbours anymore)* features nine compact walls crafted from brick, concrete, foam and metal, evoking famous barriers like the Berlin Wall and the Great Wall of China. These approachable, scaled-down structures invite visitors to climb over them, subverting the very purpose of a wall. Garaicoa's work prompts us to consider how boundaries both divide us and become lasting cultural symbols or even landmarks.

Castello di Ama

04.

Grayson Perry
A House for Essex

Wrabness, UK

Perched on the banks of the River Stour in Wrabness, Essex, this unique holiday home by artist Grayson Perry celebrates the imagined life of Julie May Cope – a fictional working class 'Essex everywoman' invented by Perry. Designed in collaboration with FAT Architecture and commissioned by Living Architecture, the house is richly decorated and fairytale-like, with a pitched, tiered roof and over 2,000 green-and-white ceramic tiles. Its design evokes both a folkloric chapel and the English Arts and Crafts movement. The exterior has the solemn presence of a chapel yet remains playful, filled with colour and patterns that reflect the distinctive character and history of Essex.

Inside, the house is designed as a series of connected rooms that build in drama and detail as you move through them. Each space offers insight into Julie's imagined biography, from her childhood to her tragic death in a motorbike accident. Perry incorporated a series of large tapestries titled *The Essex House Tapestries: The Life of Julie Cope,* which chronicle key episodes in her life from her birth in flood-hit Canvey Island to her demise in Colchester, while the façade tiles bear motifs referencing her personality and history. The artist specially commissioned artworks – ceramic reliefs, tapestries, personal objects, even a suspended motorbike – that transform the interior into an immersive, theatrical *Gesamtkunstwerk*. The artist's love of ornaments, storytelling and oral history are reflected in every aspect of this artwork.

A House for Essex is not just a place to look at art – it's an artwork you can actually stay in. Visitors can stay overnight, experiencing a day or two in the life of Julie May Cope.

ABOUT GRAYSON PERRY

Grayson Perry was born in 1960 in Chelmsford, UK. He has a rich and varied artistic practice and is renowned for his ceramic vases, elaborate tapestries and his cross-dressing public persona. Best known for blending traditional craft with biting social commentary, his work explores themes of class, identity, gender and British culture. Perry often draws inspiration from everyday life, folk-art and personal experiences, using humour and storytelling to tackle serious subjects. His distinctive style and fearless critique of social norms have made him one of the United Kingdom's most recognisable contemporary artists.

Three other artworks you can spend the night in

- **TATZU NISHI, Villa Cheminée, NANTES**
  Villa Cheminée is a habitable sculpture near the Loire river in France. Tatzu Nishi created an identical copy of a nearby power station and crowned it with a cosy one-room cottage complete with bed, kitchenette and small garden. Visitors can sleep in this surreal retreat, where they may gain a new perspective on industrial structures while enjoying panoramic views over the Loire.

- **JAMES TURRELL, House of Light, ECHIGO-TSUMARI**
  House of Light is a habitable artwork by James Turrell (p. 142) in the mountains of Echigo-Tsumari, Japan. Designed as both a traditional Japanese house and a light installation, every room reflects Turrell's lifelong exploration of perception. The highlight is a tatami room with a retractable roof that opens to the sky, allowing guests to witness the changing light from dawn to dusk. With fibre-optic features and carefully orchestrated lighting throughout, the house transforms an overnight stay into a meditative experience of living inside light itself.

- **ATELIER VAN LIESHOUT, CasAnus, KEMZEKE**
  CasAnus by Atelier Van Lieshout is a bold, immersive sculpture located at the Verbeke Foundation in Belgium. Shaped like a gigantic human digestive tract, the final section – a massive intestine ending as an 'anus' – serves as a one-room hotel, complete with a double bed, shower and toilet. The artwork playfully confronts taboos around the body and expectations about hospitality, inviting visitors to literally inhabit part of the human digestive system.

Atelier Van Lieshout, CasAnus

05.

James Lee Byars
The Spinning Oracle of Delphi

Schloss Moyland, Bedburg-Hau, Germany

The Spinning Oracle of Delphi by James Lee Byars is sited in the castle moat at Schloss Moyland, where it seems to float on the water. You cannot walk up close to it; instead, you catch glimpses of its golden form from the grassy banks around the water, where it emerges like an ancient relic rising from the surface.

The work is part of Museum Schloss Moyland's collection because of Byars's close, 15-year correspondence and friendship with German artist Joseph Beuys. This connection explains why Byars is represented at the museum with multiple works: Museum Schloss Moyland houses the world's largest collection of Beuys's art. Their exchange of ideas around ritual, transformation and participatory art resonates in Byars's piece, which invites contemplation rather than direct access.

The title '*The Spinning Oracle of Delphi*' refers to the ancient Greek sanctuary at Delphi, where people journeyed to consult the oracle, the Pythia, who delivered cryptic, often ambiguous prophecies. Just like the ancient oracle, Byars's sculpture has an air of mystery: it offers no clear narrative but asks viewers to reflect on what they seek or hope to know.

Byars chose to cover the large terracotta amphora – a pointed-bottom ancient vessel designed to store and transport wine or grain – entirely in gold leaf. The reflective gold surface elevates the amphora from a dated artefact into a timeless, ritual-like object. Gold is central to Byars's visual language: he used it not for mere decoration, but as a medium of transformation. Byars believed that gold carried spiritual weight, embodying perfection while acknowledging human fragility – it was a 'veneer' that represented an unattainable ideal. His gilded works invite contemplation of mortality, beauty and transcendence, consistent with his lifelong quest for philosophical inquiry through art.

ABOUT JAMES LEE BYARS

James Lee Byars was born in 1932 in Detroit, USA, and passed away in 1997. He was an American artist known for his minimalist, conceptual and performance-based work. Inspired by philosophy, rituals and Eastern aesthetics, he explored themes of beauty, perfection and the unknowable. He often used reflective materials like gold and marble. Byars's work blurs the line between art and spiritual experience, aiming to create moments of transcendence and provoke questions about life, death and meaning.

Schloss Moyland

Three other castles that showcase contemporary art

- **UJAZDOWSKI CASTLE CENTRE FOR CONTEMPORARY ART, WARSAW**
  This 17th-century castle in Warsaw, Poland, hosts cutting-edge international contemporary art, residencies, performances and experimental projects, with a strong focus on critical, interdisciplinary practices.

- **CASTELLO DI RIVOLI, TURIN**
  This Baroque castle near Turin (Italy) has been transformed into Italy's premier contemporary art museum, renowned for its Arte Povera collection (an Italian movement from the 1960s, where everyday, natural and fragile materials are used to oppose commercialism and abstract art) and for hosting major international exhibitions.

- **CHÂTEAU DE MONTSOREAU - MUSEUM OF CONTEMPORARY ART, LOIRE VALLEY**
  This Renaissance castle is situated on the French Loire river and is known for its major collection of conceptual art and Art & Language works (a British movement from the 1960s that pioneered conceptual art by using language and theory as an artistic medium). The Château also provides a home for contemporary avant-garde art.

Castello di Rivoli

A BAD
PLACE

Château de Montsoreau - Museum of Contemporary Art

06.

Jeff Koons
Apollo Wind Spinner

Deste Foundation Project Space Slaughterhouse, Hydra, Greece

The car-free island of Hydra is often referred to as a magical place. Despite being only 20 kilometres long and for the most part uninhabited, Hydra is home to over 300 churches, lending it a spiritual quality. The island is surrounded by the most crystal-clear, turquoise waters that, in absence of sandy beaches, you can only reach via pine tree–lined coves. There are no high-rises or resorts, no motor vehicles nor even bicycles on Hydra; deliveries are carried up from the port by donkey.

The dreamy island has long been a muse for artists, attracting painters, writers and musicians: Leonard Cohen famously met his Marianne here, adding to the island's romantic mystique. As you arrive in the port of Hydra – the island is just a two-hour ferry ride from Athens – you are greeted by the Greek god Apollo. This 9.1-metre wind spinner by Jeff Koons is installed above the Deste Foundation Project Space, a satellite of the Athens-based contemporary art centre, housed in Hydra's former slaughterhouse on the outer edge of the island.

Made of bronze to evoke an ancient quality, the sculpture reflects the awe and wonder that once filled the classical world: on calm days, it stands still, but when the wind picks up, Apollo comes to life, spinning over the Aegean Sea. Not too fast though – the spinner is set up to rotate at a slow pace, creating a meditative spin rather than rapid movement, in line with Hydra's calm energy. Koons's *Apollo Wind Spinner* bridges contemporary and ancient Greece beautifully: a modern interpretation of the god of sun, light, music, dance, poetry, truth and prophecy, right at home on the mystical island of Hydra.

ABOUT JEFF KOONS

Jeff Koons was born in 1955 in York (Pennsylvania), USA. His work is inspired by popular culture, consumerism and the everyday. He is well known for his iconic *Balloon Dog* that has been exhibited all over the world. Rising to prominence in the 1980s, he became one of the most controversial and celebrated figures in contemporary art, often blurring the boundary between fine art and mass-produced objects. His monumental sculptures invite both awe and debate about taste, value and the role of art in a consumer society.

Three other European islands with a vibrant art scene

- **MALLORCA, SPAIN**
  Mallorca offers a strong art focus, anchored by the Fundació Pilar i Joan Miró a Mallorca, where visitors can explore Joan Miró's studios and works in a setting that reflects his deep connection to the island. When visiting Mallorca, don't miss the Cathedral of Palma, known as La Seu, a Gothic landmark with architectural interventions by Antoni Gaudí.

- **CYPRUS**
  Cyprus has an evolving art scene with the contemporary art centre NiMAC presenting major exhibitions of Cypriot and international artists. Across the island, seasonal art events and fairs showcase emerging Cypriot artists, while street art throughout Cyprus's cities makes contemporary art a vital part of urban life.

- **MENORCA, SPAIN**
  The contemporary art scene in Menorca is led by gallery Hauser & Wirth Menorca, located on Isla del Rey. It features temporary exhibitions by artists such as Louise Bourgeois (p. 198), Rashid Johnson and Eduardo Chillida, as well as a sculpture trail, landscaped gardens by Piet Oudolf (p. 86) and artist residency spaces. Also in Menorca, LÔAC (Alaior Art Contemporani) opened in 2022 in Alaior, transforming a historic building into a contemporary art museum hosting rotating exhibitions with both Spanish and international artists.

Fundació Pilar i Joan Miró a Mallorca

VOYAGEZ LEGEREMENT

07.

Jenny Holzer
Truisms

Furka Pass, Switzerland

The Furka Pass trail, marked as Route 51 on the Swiss national trail system, takes hikers along a historic transit route, following well-maintained former military and mule paths. Typically completed in two days, the high-altitude route offers panoramic views across the Alps. Around half an hour's walk from the Furka Pass itself, the words 'IMPARA LE COSE DA ZERO' ('LEARN THINGS FROM SCRATCH') have been carved into a boulder.

This text is an artwork by Jenny Holzer and is part of her ongoing body of work called '*Truisms*' – poetic and sometimes provocative statements that reflect on different aspects of life and society. Holzer first brought these phrases into the world in the late 1970s and early '80s, bypassing museums by placing them in public spaces in New York City, using stickers, T-shirts and posters. In 1980, she famously posted an LED sign in Times Square reading 'ABUSE OF POWER COMES AS NO SURPRISE'. To this day, she continues to use the public space as her canvas, projecting critical texts and poetry onto buildings, or sharing them on LED screens mounted onto moving trucks.

But how did this particular artwork by Holzer end up on this mountain? Between 1983 and 1999, Swiss gallerist Marc Hostettler invited around 60 artists, including Marina Abramović and Ulay, Joseph Beuys, James Lee Byars (p. 38) and Jenny Holzer, to participate in Furk'art – an initiative that encouraged artists to engage directly with the spectacular yet unforgiving mountain landscape. Holzer created 12 *Truisms* along the Furka Pass, each carved into boulders near mountain streams.

After the gallerist sold the property, a foundation was established by its new owner (the heir to Ricola – the famous Swiss herbal cough drops) to care for the artworks that remain on the Furka Pass. There are few left behind, as most of the works created during Furk'art were performative and therefore temporary. Besides Holzer's *Truisms*, Daniel Buren's striped shutters still adorn the façade of the Hotel Furkablick, which is part of the property and was renovated in the late 1980s by star architect Rem Koolhaas's firm OMA. Unfortunately, you cannot book a room there – it is in use during the summer months as a residency for artists and architects, who occasionally install new artworks in the area: in the summer of 2024, Guillaume Bijl's intervention was unveiled. Bijl mounted a sign on the hotel exterior, mysteriously reading 'À VENDRE' ('FOR SALE').

ABOUT JENNY HOLZER

Jenny Holzer was born in 1950 in Gallipolis, USA. She is a conceptual and installation artist who works primarily with text in public space, addressing social and political injustice. Her practice spans a range of media, including electronic signs, stone, paintings, billboards and printed materials.

Josette Taramarcaz, Arche (Verbier 3-D Foundation)

Three other must-visit places in Switzerland

- **FONDATION BEYELER, BASEL**
  Fondation Beyeler was born from the private collection of Ernst and Hildy Beyeler. The museum is surrounded by a park and water lily pond, blending modern art with nature. In the gardens you will find works by Ellsworth Kelly, Alexander Calder and Thomas Schütte.

- **VERBIER 3-D FOUNDATION, VERBIER**
  At 2,300 metres in the Alps, the Verbier 3-D Foundation operates as a research-driven sculpture park and residency, producing site-specific installations rooted in landscape and environmental exploration.

- **FONDATION PIERRE GIANADDA, MARTIGNY**
  The Fondation Pierre Gianadda is home to an extensive sculpture park with works by more than 40 artists, including Niki de Saint Phalle (p. 76), Joan Miró and Auguste Rodin, set against a backdrop of vineyards and mountains.

Rana Begum, No. 1387 Fence (Verbier 3-D Foundation)

08.

Jeppe Hein
Path of Emotions

Fondation Carmignac, Porquerolles, France

Tucked away on the tiny but beautiful island of Porquerolles is the Fondation Carmignac. Inside its villa, you will find contemporary art exhibitions. In the lush natural gardens, which stretch over 15 hectares, you can discover 16 outdoor sculptures thoughtfully placed among native plants of the Hyères region.

Reflecting this natural beauty and the breathtaking views of the island and the surrounding sea is Jeppe Hein's installation *Path of Emotions*. This mirrored labyrinth, inspired by the shape of the local yarrow plant, will draw you right in. Once inside, you may find yourself disoriented by the interplay between the sculpture's fixed height and the shifting levels of the walking path. The horizon remains constant, but the landscape seems to move, offering new perspectives – not least on yourself – as you see yourself reflected in its surfaces.

This focus on experience is central to Hein's work. His works blur the line between art and life, drawing you in and making you part of the artwork itself. Around the world, he has created pieces that invite participation and play, from his *Modified Social Benches*, which transform the simple act of sitting into a conscious, shared experience, to his interactive fountains that challenge visitors to interact with shifting walls of water.

ABOUT JEPPE HEIN

Jeppe Hein was born in 1974 in Copenhagen, Denmark. Hein is known for his humorous and interactive artworks. Often combining elements of sculpture, architecture and performance, his works transform ordinary situations into playful encounters. From mirrored labyrinths to benches that twist and curve, Hein creates environments that heighten awareness, spark curiosity and turn the audience into an essential part of the artwork.

NILS-UDO, La Couvée

Other things to see in the sculpture garden at Fondation Carmignac

- **ED RUSCHA, Sea of Desire**

  Upon arriving at Fondation Carmignac, visitors are greeted by a large billboard reading 'Sea of Desire'. This work by Ed Ruscha acts as a portal to California, a place the artist has long admired for its distinctive light. Using the familiar language of American roadside billboards, here set on the island of Porquerolles against the backdrop of pine trees, the piece invites visitors to leave the everyday behind as they enter Fondation Carmignac.

- **ADRIÁN VILLAR ROJAS, The Most Beautiful of All Mothers (XII)**

  A bison stands in the gardens of the Fondation Carmignac, conjured by Adrián Villar Rojas as a symbol of a disappearing world. Straddling the line between fiction and reality, it carries remnants of the past: animals, objects and organic elements, including feathers from the pheasants that roam these grounds.

- **NILS-UDO, La Couvée**

  Don't miss the five giant eggs made of white Carrara marble by NILS-UDO. Nestled among the trees, the sculptural eggs, named *La Couvée* (the Brood), bring to mind both shelter and refuge, while inviting viewers to imagine what immense creature might one day hatch from these enormous eggs.

Adrián Villar Rojas, The Most Beautiful of All Mothers (XII)

09.

Laure Prouvost

Touching To Sea You Through Our Extremities

Beaufort Sculpture Park, De Panne, Belgium

It is not necessarily surprising to encounter a sea creature washed up on the beach: you will often find jellyfish, crabs and occasionally an octopus on the shoreline. The octopus that appears to have been stranded on the beach in the Belgian seaside town of De Panne, however, is not an ordinary one. First, there's its scale: it appears huge, even as parts of it are buried under the sandy beach. Second, this peculiar octopus is holding objects from the human world: a plug, a lamp, a telescope and other instruments. And on closer inspection, you will see that the octopus is host not only to mussels that have attached themselves to its skin, but also to human breasts. On top of all of that, the octopus is holding a flag on which are written the poetic words 'Ideally you would sea where to go'.

These fantastical elements are recurring themes in Laure Prouvost's work: she is fascinated with the octopus – having nine brains, three hearts, eight tentacles and blue blood – and has used its figure before in glass sculptures, oil paintings and watercolours. Here, its tentacles symbolise the idea of finding your way; the tools with which the octopus is equipped are helping it do so.

Breasts are also a recurring theme in Prouvost's work and a way to honour female artists and other role models, often in a humorous way – breasts are not just a symbol of nourishment, comfort, care or sensuality; they are also comical in Prouvost's eyes. Lastly, playing with language is central to Prouvost's work: she likes to strip words of their meaning or reinterpret them: here, she deliberately uses the word 'sea' incorrectly, yet it makes perfect sense.

ABOUT LAURE PROUVOST

Laure Prouvost was born in 1978 in Croix-Lille, France. She is known for her immersive installations, where images, sound, language and objects come together in absurdist and poetic ways. She draws inspiration from her own memories (often of her grandparents), from everyday life as a mother and artist, as well as from the complexities of society.

> **'The octopus represents the animal and physical connection that we have lost. We are different protagonists in this world and the tentacles connect us, blend our personalities and our different cultures.'**
>
> Laure Prouvost

Three other must-visit art sites in Belgium

- **DANIEL BUREN, Le vent souffle où il veut, NIEUWPOORT**
  Prouvost's artwork is part of the Beaufort Triennial: a triannual outdoor art exhibition along the Belgian coast. Various artworks from the Triennial remain as permanent works. You can find more fantastic(al) artworks in Nieuwpoort, such as a field of cheerful, striped flags by Daniel Buren (p. 28), aptly titled *Le vent souffle où il veut (The wind blows wherever it likes).*

- **MIDDELHEIM MUSEUM, ANTWERP**
  In the mood for more sculpture, but in a green setting? Visit Middelheim Museum, a free art park in Antwerp where art and nature come together. Among the trees and lawns you will encounter works by Ai Weiwei (p. 120), Barbara Hepworth and Alexander Calder, as well as temporary exhibitions by contemporary artists.

- **KANAAL, WIJNEGEM**
  In the small city of Wijnegem, about 20 minutes outside of Antwerp, you will find Kanaal, a residential, commercial and cultural hub, housed in a former distillery from 1857. Inside Kanaal, the Axel & May Vervoordt Foundation (yes, star interior designer, curator, antiques dealer and gallerist Axel Vervoordt, whose famous clients include the likes of Sting, Kim Kardashian and Robert De Niro) has installed several awe-inspiring permanent works by artists such as Anish Kapoor, James Turrell (p. 142) and Marina Abramović.

Kanaal

10.

Marc Quinn
All of Nature Flows Through Us

Kistefos Museum, Jevnaker, Norway

Nestled within a lush forest and surrounded by a winding river lies the Kistefos sculpture park, a site that offers a seamless blend of contemporary art, architecture and nature. Scattered throughout the museum's outdoor grounds, you can explore over 50 art installations by internationally renowned artists, most pieces created specifically for this unique environment.

Marc Quinn's *All of Nature Flows Through Us* is a large bronze sculpture of an iris that combines portraiture and landscape. Positioned in the rushing waters of the Randselva river that runs through the sculpture park, the eye – modelled after the iris of Christen Sveaas, owner and founder of Kistefos Museum – displays the intricate patterns of the iris, unique to each person.

The sculpture's surface interacts with light and shadow, giving it a dynamic presence. At its centre, a hollowed-out pupil allows the river to flow through, merging a small detail of human anatomy with the overpowering force of nature. The water's movement through the eye underscores the idea that we are not separate from nature, but rather an intrinsic part of its continuous flow.

Quinn reinterprets the traditional genre of portraiture, using the eye as a bridge between humanity and the environment. In an era dominated by visual culture, the artwork serves as both a literal and symbolic lens, urging viewers to observe, reflect and recognise their responsibility in preserving the natural world.

ABOUT MARC QUINN

Marc Quinn was born in 1964 in London, UK. He is known for his explorations of the human body and the relationship between art and science. Quinn first gained international recognition in the early 1990s as part of the Young British Artists (YBAs) movement. Quinn's practice spans sculpture, painting and installation, often incorporating unconventional materials such as DNA, blood, water and flowers. His iconic and oversized sculptures challenge perceptions of beauty, physicality and human fragility. Quinn's art provokes dialogue on topics such as body politics, climate change and technology. He continues to push boundaries, questioning what it means to be human in a rapidly changing world.

Yayoi Kusama, Shine of Life

Other things to see at Kistefos Museum

- **BJARKE INGELS, The Twist**
  The centrepiece of Kistefos is *The Twist*, a striking building designed by Bjarke Ingels that doubles as a bridge and a gallery. Its twisted shape spirals elegantly over the Randselva river, creating both a practical crossing and an artwork in its own right. With reflective surfaces and flowing lines, the structure constantly changes character as the light and weather shift. Inside, *The Twist* hosts exhibitions of international contemporary art, making it an unforgettable museum space.

- **TONY OURSLER, Scat Skat Skatt**
  At Kistefos, art truly appears everywhere – yes, even in the bathrooms. Answering the challenge to create the world's most spectacular toilets, American artist Tony Oursler transformed *The Twist*'s public toilets into a multimedia artwork. Known for his surreal, animated projections and playful approach, Oursler fills the space with sound, light and unexpected images. Commissioned by founder Christen Sveaas, the installation ensures that even your most private moments at Kistefos become part of the artistic experience.

- **YAYOI KUSAMA, Shine of Life**
  Rising out of the dark water, Yayoi Kusama's *Shine of Life* surprises visitors with a dozen bright red, polka-dotted tentacles. The playful shapes seem at once cheerful and slightly monstrous, reaching towards the sky as if alive. Surrounded by forest and water, the work creates a vivid contrast with its natural setting. Kusama (p. 208) designed the piece especially for Kistefos, bringing her signature patterns and sense of wonder to the Norwegian landscape.

Bjarke Ingels, The Twist

Bjarke Ingels, The Twist

11.

Martin Creed
Work No. 2792 and Work No. 1086

Museum Voorlinden, Wassenaar, The Netherlands

A beautiful garden designed by Piet Oudolf (p. 86) frames Museum Voorlinden, located in the natural dune landscape near the North Sea coast in the Netherlands. Within this garden, you will find a work by Martin Creed that is hardly recognisable as an artwork: *Work No. 2792* consists of four trees that appear to be simply part of the garden. However, this is a conceptual work, rooted in Creed's lived experience as a person who is plagued by fears and deals with them by attempting to establish order – the way he numbers each of his artworks is exemplary of this need for structure.

To create this artwork, the museum received a short set of instructions: select four different kinds of trees, each clearly distinct, and plant them in a row from small to large at equal distances. The work raises the question whether order can ever truly be imposed: trees grow at different rates, subject to animal activity, weather and seasons – one may outgrow the other, breaking the carefully planned sequence. Creed's *Work No. 2792* is perhaps not so much about achieving order, but about (accepting) the impossibility of it.

This work is closely related to another work by Martin Creed that at one point was placed by a small pond in the Voorlinden garden, reading in white neon letters 'EVERYTHING IS GOING TO BE ALRIGHT'. According to Creed, this phrase was said to him by a friend and offered him great comfort at the time. He has been repeating it since 1999 in the form of this neon work, installing it in cities around the world (including on the façade of the Modern One, part of the National Galleries of Scotland in Edinburgh). It is almost as if he is willing the phrase into existence by using it as a mantra. Yet, the phrase can also be interpreted as a tongue-in-cheek cliché – Creed's work often carries a thread of humour. Is it ironic or comforting? You decide.

ABOUT MARTIN CREED

Martin Creed was born in 1968 in Wakefield, UK. He works across film, installation, performance and sculpture, using whatever medium feels right for the idea at hand. His practice is marked by a mix of humour and structure, often using everyday actions, objects or sounds to highlight the beauty and absurdity of the ordinary. By stripping things down to their simplest form, Creed invites viewers to reconsider how they perceive the world around them.

Piet Oudolf, Garden Voorlinden

Neon artworks in public spaces worth a visit

- **TRACEY EMIN, I Want My Time With You, LONDON**
  Tracey Emin's 20-metre hot pink, neon sculpture underneath the clock in London's St. Pancras station (UK) reads 'I Want My Time With You', welcoming travellers with a message of love. Worth noting: in this case, Emin (p. 104) did not direct this message at a person per se, but at Europe on the brink of Brexit.

- **DAN FLAVIN, Installation at Richmond Hall, HOUSTON**
  Dan Flavin's neon works at Richmond Hall in Houston (USA), part of the impressive Menil Collection, include green fluorescent lights tracing the building's exterior edges and a diagonal arrangement of daylight lamps in the lobby. These works lead up to the spectacular main hall, where an immersive experience unfolds through a sequence of coloured tubes in pink, yellow, green and blue, punctuated by black light.

- **DANIEL BUREN, Les Anneaux, NANTES**
  In the Parc des Chantiers on the western tip of Île de Nantes (France), artist Daniel Buren (p. 28) created *Les Anneaux* to highlight the unique perspective at the tip of the island. The 18 large, red, blue and green neon rings, aligned along the quay, frame views of the city's industrial architecture and the Loire river. Do visit at night!

Tracey Emin, I Want My Time With You

12.

Martin Puryear
Meditation in a Beech Wood

Wanås Konst, Knislinge, Sweden

Set deep among the towering trees of a Swedish beech forest, Martin Puryear's *Meditation in a Beech Wood* rises nearly five metres tall like a quiet guardian of craft and contemplation. Built entirely of thatch – hundreds of thousands of carefully bundled reed stems – the sculpture has a rounded, organic silhouette inspired by the seated form of a Buddha. Though visitors cannot enter it, the work radiates a sense of shelter and softness, which is a rare accomplishment given its monumental scale and rigid material.

Puryear was captivated by the region's long tradition of thatching, which he first glimpsed from a train window on an early visit to Sweden. For centuries, thatch has offered practical protection, shaping architecture in this region. When Puryear was invited by the Wanås Foundation, dedicated to contemporary art and known for housing the collection's 70+ site-specific works in nature, he chose to honour this heritage, working closely with experienced craftspeople. Mastery of thatch demands deep knowledge and patient technique, and his collaborators feared his complex, curving design was impossible in such a stubbornly traditional material.

But Puryear persisted, eventually partnering with an expert thatcher to realise his vision.

The sculpture's making was an exercise in craft: Puryear developed functional maquettes, sawing them apart to study cross-sections and design the internal wooden frame that would support the thatching – a process reflecting his lifelong commitment to understanding materials from the inside out. *Meditation in a Beech Wood* embodies his ethos: it is both an homage to local and traditional crafts and an abstract, universal gesture of contemplation and protection. A small wooden maquette of *Meditation in a Beech Wood* can be found in the collection of Storm King Art Center.

ABOUT MARTIN PURYEAR

Martin Puryear was born in 1941 in Washington, DC, USA. Puryear is a sculptor celebrated for his poetic, minimalist forms shaped with refined craftsmanship. He is inspired by traditional techniques, from Scandinavian woodwork to skills he encountered during his Peace Corps service in Sierra Leone. Often working with wood, wire and other natural materials, Puryear creates subtle, evocative sculptures that suggest universal ideas of shelter and freedom. His distinctive style is marked by organic, familiar shapes rendered with artisanal precision.

Three other must-see artworks in Wanås Konst

- **JENNY HOLZER, Wanås Wall**
  While wandering the forest seeking a site for her *Truisms* (p. 48), Jenny Holzer discovered an 18th-century drystone wall and engraved a series of her iconic one-liners, such as 'All things are delicately interconnected', into the ancient stones, integrating text with history and landscape.

- **MARINA ABRAMOVIĆ, The Hunt Chair for Animal Spirits**
  This 12-metre sculpture by Marina Abramović takes its form from a hunter's high seat, its frame crowned with racks of deer and moose antlers. The tower feels at once archaic and ceremonial – a beacon, a warning, a memorial.

- **ROBERT WILSON, A House for Edwin Denby**
  Set among the beech trees, this small house cannot be entered, but visitors can peek inside through the window into an almost empty room that holds only an open book and bare light bulbs. A solemn, organ-like sound fills the air as a voice reads poetry by Edwin Denby, American poet and dance critic.

Robert Wilson, A House for Edwin Denby

Wanås Konst

13.

Niki de Saint Phalle
The Tarot Garden

Capalbio, Italy

Il Giardino dei Tarocchi (The Tarot Garden) in Tuscany is the life's work of Niki de Saint Phalle. Beginning in the late 1970s, she devoted more than two decades to its creation, imagining a sculpture park where art, nature and spirituality meet. Drawing inspiration from Antoni Gaudí's Parc Güell in Barcelona, Spain, among others, she envisioned the project as an homage to esotericism.

Tarot originated in Italy in the mid-15th century, created as an elaborate card game called *tarocchi*, for the elite. Fortune-telling with tarot developed much later, in the 18th century. *The Tarot Garden* is filled with monumental figures inspired by the Major Arcana, the 22 cards that symbolise archetypal themes, spiritual paths and key lessons in life. Saint Phalle reimagined figures from these cards, such as *The Magician*, *The High Priestess* and *The Empress*, in her unmistakable style of vibrant colour and bold forms. For her, these archetypes provided a universal symbolic language, a way to speak about human experience, transformation and the mysteries of life. The sculptures are immersive environments: visitors can enter the sculptures and walk through them.

Saint Phalle invested her own resources in the project to ensure its independence, financing it through her art sales and creating a perfume line. She chose to live inside *The Empress* – a monumental sculpture that served as her personal residence and a fully functional home with a kitchen, bedroom and bathroom – during parts of the construction. She built the garden with the help of a loyal team of friends and artists, including her husband, Jean Tinguely.

ABOUT NIKI DE SAINT PHALLE

Niki de Saint Phalle was born in France in 1930 and later lived between the United States and Europe before passing away in 2002. She worked as a fashion model and studied theatre before turning to art. From the mid-1960s, she gained international recognition for her vividly painted *Nanas*: bold, joyful depictions of women, which celebrated femininity while challenging social norms by rejecting traditional ideals of female beauty and passivity. Her practice often drew on personal experience and explored themes of trauma, feminism and freedom.

Niki de Saint Phalle, Fontaine aux Nanas

Three other outdoor artworks by Niki de Saint Phalle

- **Queen Califia's Magical Circle, ESCONDIDO**
  In Escondido, California, lies *Queen Califia's Magical Circle* – Niki de Saint Phalle's only sculpture garden in the United States. Completed in 2003 from her original sketches, this dazzling fantasy world is created entirely from mosaic tiles. At its centre is Queen Califia herself, seated on a five-legged eagle, surrounded by fierce, colourful figures and a giant snake wall that coils around the garden.

- **Sun God, SAN DIEGO**
  At the Stuart Collection at the University of California San Diego, Niki de Saint Phalle's *Sun God* – a multicoloured bird made of polyester and fibreglass – has become a beloved campus icon. Beyond lending its name to the annual Sun God Festival, the sculpture has been regularly dressed up by students over the years, who have left it sporting everything from sunglasses to graduation caps.

- **The Stravinsky Fountain, PARIS**
  The Stravinsky Fountain by Niki de Saint Phalle and Jean Tinguely, right in front of Centre Pompidou in Paris (France), consists of 16 colourful, moving sculptures that splash and whirl in homage to composer Igor Stravinsky. Although the commission was first given to Tinguely alone, he insisted that Saint Phalle's vibrant figures join his dark mechanical forms, turning the fountain into a true collaboration.

'Painting calmed the chaos that shook my soul.'

Niki de Saint Phalle

14.

Olafur Eliasson
Our glacial perspective

Grawand Mountain, Italy

High on Grawand, a mountain in Italy's South Tyrol, Olafur Eliasson's artwork *Our glacial perspective* emerges from the rocky Alpine landscape. After a steep ascent – 3,212 metres above sea level – by glacier cable car, a walk along the winding mountain path awaits. The walkway is cut along a glacier-shaped ridge, providing panoramic views of the Alps. As you walk, nine steel gates rise before you, alternating black and white, each spaced with precise care to suggest the rhythm of Earth's long ice ages and the warmer periods between. These elegant minimalist frames slice the landscape into segments of time, urging the viewer to see geology as a series of vast, slow cycles.

The path ends at a large installation that looms over the mountainside. Here, steel rings interlock with small squares of blue-tinted glass that catch and colour the Alpine light. The pavilion feels both ancient and futuristic – a kind of deserted open-air observatory suspended above the glacier. Looking through the rings, you see the sun's arc tracked with scientific precision: the outer ring marks the summer solstice, the middle ring the equinoxes, and the inner the winter solstice. The glass segments act like a giant clock face, dividing the view into time zones of 15 arc minutes each and letting you roughly tell the time by reading the sunlight.

The colour of the glass is no random choice: its deep blues evoke the cyanometer, the old instrument used to measure the blueness of the sky, while also recalling the cold, translucent glow of glacial ice. Framed against the receding glacier, the pavilion becomes a stark reminder of environmental fragility. Eliasson's design doesn't just offer a scenic lookout – it transforms the mountain into a vast timeline, where you literally walk through Earth's climate history.

ABOUT OLAFUR ELIASSON

Olafur Eliasson was born in 1967 in Copenhagen, Denmark. He is an Icelandic–Danish artist known for large-scale installations that play with light, perception and natural elements. He often draws inspiration from landscapes, weather and scientific tools, exploring how we experience our environment. His work uses materials like water, fog, glass and light to create immersive spaces that invite reflection on nature and climate change. Eliasson aims to make viewers more aware of their surroundings and of the planet's vulnerability.

Three tips for nearby sites

- **GLACIER HOTEL GRAWAND**
  Stay at the Glacier Hotel Grawand, right next to *Our glacial perspectives,* and see the artwork transform throughout the day. From dawn's soft glow to the sharp midday sun and the fading evening light, each moment reveals new tones of blue.

- **ÖTZI**
  Just minutes from *Our glacial perspective,* Ötzi the Iceman was discovered in 1991 on the Italy–Austria border. This Copper Age man lived over 5,300 years ago and was preserved in glacial ice, offering a rare glimpse of ancient Alpine life.

- **MUZEUM SUSCH**
  Tucked deep in the Swiss Alps, Muzeum Susch is set in a former monastery complex carved into the mountains. Founded by private collector Grażyna Kulczyk, it showcases contemporary art surrounded by ancient Alpine rock structures.

Iceman Ötzi Peak

15.

Piet Oudolf
Oudolf Field

Hauser & Wirth Somerset, Bruton, UK

Can a garden be an artwork in and of itself? In the eyes of global gallery Hauser & Wirth, the answer is yes. And we wholeheartedly agree. The Oudolf Field at Hauser & Wirth in Bruton, located in the rolling, green county of Somerset, offers a lively landscape, encouraging contemplation and reflection. Rather than offering dramatic spectacle, the garden unfolds gradually. In his design, Oudolf mixes colour, texture, structure, height and size, much as a painter would in a meticulously composed oil painting. The careful layering of colourful blooms adds depth and vibrancy, while the varied plant textures create richness and rhythm. The gently waving grasses create an opaque effect reminiscent of a painter's brushstroke.

The garden also exhibits outdoor sculptures from artists featured in the adjoining exhibition space of Hauser & Wirth. We would be remiss to not also mention the farm shop located on the grounds, with an excellent selection of local, seasonal, fresh produce and great souvenirs such as locally produced gin and honey.

Piet Oudolf has designed other public gardens as well, such as the famous High Line in New York City (USA), built upon obsolete overground railroad tracks in the Chelsea district. The Hauser & Wirth gallery in Menorca, Spain, also features an Oudolf garden, as does Museum Voorlinden in the Dutch town of Wassenaar and the Serpentine Galleries located within Kensington Gardens in London (UK).

ABOUT PIET OUDOLF

Piet Oudolf was born in 1944 in Haarlem, the Netherlands. His landscape designs are inspired by nature, time and art. Oudolf's signature style mixes grasses, perennials and garden beds, meant to look beautiful in any season. For Oudolf, it is important that a garden is appealing not just during peak flowering season, but also before and after; his work embraces the life cycle and appreciates bloom and decay equally.

Other places to visit in Somerset

- **BATH**
  The nearby city of Bath can be described as a living museum. Come for its stately 18th-century Georgian architecture – known for its symmetry, proportion and classical details inspired by Greek and Roman architecture – and stay for its art museums such as the Holburne Museum and the Victoria Art Gallery, both offering a historical collection as well as contemporary art exhibitions.

- **GLASTONBURY**
  Glastonbury, known for its legendary music festival, is also home to the Glastonbury Mural Trail, featuring over 70 murals by more than 50 different artists. While you're there, don't skip the Glastonbury Tor: a landmark dating back to the 15th century, with sweeping views of the Somerset Levels, Dorset, Wiltshire and Wales.

- **BABINGTON HOUSE**
  Looking for a place to stay? Luxurious Babington House, part of the Soho House group, occupies a manor built in 1705 in the heart of Somerset. Around the house, you will find over 40 contemporary artworks of well-known artists as well as emerging talent, celebrating local artists such as Daisy Parris and Sam Taylor-Johnson.

Bath

16.

Pipilotti Rist
Nordic Pixel Forest

Ekebergparken, Oslo, Norway

Nordic Pixel Forest by Pipilotti Rist is a video and sound installation composed of glowing orbs that are suspended among the trees of Oslo's Ekebergparken Sculpture Park. Spanning a woven net of steel cables roughly seven metres above the ground, it contains 24,000 LED lights clustered into 3,600 delicate translucent 'pixels' that glow, shift and breathe with colour. The light radiating through the orbs is like a projection of individual pixels in an abstracted video. Rist describes the installation as an exploded television screen that invites the audience to move between the scattered pixels and become part of the moving image.

The installation can be experienced throughout the year and reveals varying qualities at different times of the day. Visitors are free to wander between hundreds of softly glowing orbs, each pulsing with changing hues – icy blues, luminous greens, pale pinks. From below, it can look like a modern aurora: pixelated and structured, yet alive with motion. The lights play with perception. Up close, their modular design feels technological; seen from afar, the soft, muted colours become almost painterly. Occasionally, the bulbs fade nearly to darkness before bursting into new palettes, inviting you to linger and discover the work again and again.

There is no single viewpoint for this installation. The experience is shaped by movement: crunching over the woodland paths, glimpsing light through branches and feeling the cold air all intensify the vivid glow. This openness is central to Rist's artistic approach. Known for sensuous environments that dissolve the line between viewer and artwork, she often uses indoor video projections to sculpt space. Here, she exchanges the white cube for a living forest, letting technology heighten awareness of the landscape rather than overshadow it. In *Nordic Pixel Forest*, Rist extends her signature strategies to the outdoors, allowing the installation to become one with Ekeberg's ancient trees and rocky slopes.

ABOUT PIPILOTTI RIST

Pipilotti Rist was born in 1962 in Grabs, Switzerland. She is mostly known for large, colourful video installations. She takes inspiration from nature, the female body, pop music and advertising. Her work explores themes like intimacy, sexuality and point of view. Rist's visual style features bright, saturated colours, close-up shots and slow, flowing movement, often with layered sounds. She transforms walls, floors and even forests into glowing, dreamlike environments. Her art invites visitors to walk through, look closely and feel part of the experience, breaking down the barrier between artwork and viewer.

'I am interested in the combination of nature and technology; these are not two different things.'

Pipilotti Rist

Three other artworks to see in Oslo

- **TRACEY EMIN, The Mother**
  Tracey Emin's (p. 104) *The Mother* is a nine-metre-tall bronze sculpture located outside Oslo's MUNCH museum. It shows a woman kneeling, her arms wrapped protectively around an invisible child. Facing the fjord, the figure symbolises care and guardianship, paying tribute to the strength and tenderness of motherhood.

- **EDVARD MUNCH, The Scream**
  Three versions of Edvard Munch's *The Scream* – a painting, a drawing and a print – are shown together in one room at Oslo's MUNCH museum. The iconic image of a ghostlike figure under a swirling sky symbolises anxiety and despair. To protect it from light damage, the original oil-and-tempera painting is only revealed for a few minutes each hour, adding drama to the viewing experience.

- **FUJIKO NAKAYA, Pathfinder #18700 Oslo – Blindern**
  This fog sculpture by Fujiko Nakaya (p. 192) in Ekebergparken, near Pipilotti Rist's work, uses hundreds of micro-nozzles to create drifting clouds of mist that respond to the surrounding weather conditions. The installation can only be experienced during the warmer months and as the sculpture is activated several times a day, visitors are advised to check the park's schedule in advance.

Edvard Munch, The Scream

Fujiko Nakaya, Pathfinder #18700 Oslo – Blindern

ICI
REPOSENT
LES SECRETS
DES PROMENEURS

17.

Sophie Calle
Dead End

Château La Coste, Le Puy-Sainte-Réparade, France

Bringing together art, nature, wine and food, Château La Coste is a dream destination for any art lover. Spread across 200 hectares, it offers a hotel, several restaurants, multiple indoor exhibition spaces and a vineyard. But its highlight? The sculpture park, showcasing site-specific works by over 35 artists, such as Louise Bourgeois (p. 198), Richard Serra (p. 204) and Yoko Ono (p. 108). Be sure to wear comfortable shoes, as it takes at least two hours to explore the artworks scattered across the estate.

Inside the sculpture park, a wooden sign reading 'Dead End', at a fork in a long, winding path, steers you to the left. Continuing along the path, you encounter a small gold-coloured metal box holding paper and pencils and inviting you to write down a secret. You may experience mixed feelings: nervous jitters, a moment of introspection, wondering whether you are in the mood to take it seriously and what it all means. As you write down your secret, perhaps you feel a sense of relief in trusting your secret to paper, a secret you may have never allowed yourself to acknowledge, or a secret that you have carried with you.

At the end of the path stands a tombstone engraved with 'Ici reposent les secrets des promeneurs' ('Here lie the secrets of the wanderers'), with a slot for you to leave your secret behind. The artist's promise is clear: your secrets will remain here, buried and forever sealed within this poetic work, safely guarded and never retrieved. Perhaps you will find you tread a little lighter on your way back.

ABOUT SOPHIE CALLE

Sophie Calle was born in 1953 in Paris, France. Artists like Calle are hard to define. Whether working in installation, photography, books or video, she produces artworks that are as conceptual as they are poetic and deeply personal, often blending fact and fiction, art and life.

‘Art is a way of taking distance. The pathological or therapeutic aspects exist, but just as catalysts.’

Sophie Calle

Other artworks to see at Château La Coste

- **PAUL MATISSE, Meditation Bell**
  Many of the artworks in Château La Coste's sculpture garden invite moments of reflection and contemplation. This is especially true of Paul Matisse's *Meditation Bell* – a seemingly simple structure that is, in fact, technically intricate. And yes, you are welcome to ring the bell.

- **TRACEY EMIN, Self-Portrait: Cat Inside a Barrel**
  You might wonder how Tracey Emin's *Self-Portrait: Cat Inside a Barrel* is a self-portrait at all. The work consists of a walkway high in the trees, leading to a small platform with a barrel you can peek into (spoiler: there really is a cat inside). Emin (p. 104) leaves its meaning open to interpretation, offering only this hint: in her eyes, a self-portrait isn't necessarily about how she sees herself, but about how she feels.

- **TADAO ANDO, Chapel, AND JEAN-MICHEL OTHONIEL, La Grande Croix Rouge**
  At the highest point of the estate, Tadao Ando – the architect behind Château La Coste's entrance and art centre – designed a chapel with a sweeping view of the grounds and surrounding countryside. The chapel is dark, except for small openings behind the altar that allow natural light to filter in. Beside the chapel stands *La Grande Croix Rouge*, a large wine-red glass cross by Jean-Michel Othoniel.

Paul Matisse, Meditation Bell

Château La Coste

18.

Tracey Emin
I Lay Here For You

Jupiter Artland, Wilkieston, Scotland

Jupiter Artland is a contemporary sculpture garden in Wilkieston near Edinburgh, where artworks by many well-known artists from the United Kingdom (such as Marc Quinn (p. 60), Antony Gormley (p. 180), Anish Kapoor and Phyllida Barlow) are placed amid meadows and woodlands. It is easy to see why Tracey Emin fell for this particular spot when she was invited to create an artwork for Jupiter Artland. Following the winding paths through the woodlands of the approximately 50-hectare park, you come upon her sculpture, nestled among beech trees: a female figure, cast in bronze, stretching around six metres in length.

Her presence feels both powerful and intimate. As you walk up to her, it feels like you are stumbling upon a private moment. Unlike the usual upright pose of sculpted women, she lies face down, her body arranged in a way that feels private and a bit uncomfortable. It may leave you wondering, Did she fall, is she resting, or, as the title *I Lay Here For You* suggests, is she waiting for a lover, or simply for love?

The surface, first modelled in clay before being cast in bronze, retains the marks of Emin's hands, her touch visible across the folds of the body and the softness of the limbs. Up close, the sculpture is breathtaking in its vulnerability – a rare example of a work so moving that it is felt as deeply as it is seen.

ABOUT TRACEY EMIN

Tracey Emin was born in 1963 in London, UK. Her work is defined by its emotional, raw and deeply personal character. Emin, not shying away from painful or taboo topics, explores grief, loss, love, sex and the female body with unflinching honesty, using self-portraiture and nudes as recurring themes. Alongside her sculptural and painted works, she is also well known for her neon text pieces, which express her innermost thoughts and feelings.

'There should be something revelatory about art. It should be totally creative and open doors for new thoughts and experiences.'

Tracey Emin

Other things to do in Edinburgh

- **FRUITMARKET**
  Don't miss Fruitmarket, a free public space for contemporary art in the heart of Edinburgh, championing contemporary Scottish and international artists alike. It also boasts an excellent café and bookshop – and a sound installation by Martin Creed (p. 66) inside its lift.

- **THE SCOTSMAN STEPS**
  Take your time to walk the Scotsman Steps, a spiralling pedestrian staircase linking the North Bridge and Waverley Station's Market Street entrance. The structure was originally built between 1899 and 1902 as part of *The Scotsman* newspaper building. In 2010, Fruitmarket Gallery commissioned – again – Martin Creed to reimagine the landmark steps. Creed created *Work No. 1059,* cladding each of the 104 steps in a different type of marble from quarries around the world. In Creed's words, 'stepping on the different marble steps is like walking through the world'.

- **THE MODERN SCULPTURE GARDEN**
  You will find more Tracey Emin and more Martin Creed in the sculpture garden of the Modern, part of the National Galleries of Scotland, alongside works by Rachel Whiteread, Joan Miró and Barbara Hepworth.

Edinburgh

19.

Yoko Ono
IMAGINE PEACE TOWER

Viðey Island, Iceland

IMAGINE PEACE TOWER is an impressive outdoor art installation by Yoko Ono, located on Viðey Island near Reykjavík, Iceland. To visit it, you take a short boat ride from the mainland to the island. When the lights of *IMAGINE PEACE TOWER* are off, you see an understated white stone monument. The base is inscribed in 24 languages with the words 'IMAGINE PEACE'. Without the stark beam of light piercing the sky, the work feels like a traditional monument for commemoration and remembrance.

But its meaning runs deeper: wishes are collected from Ono's *Wish Tree* series around the world and connected with *IMAGINE PEACE TOWER*. The Wish Trees invite visitors to write down their hopes and dreams and hang them in the branches. By connecting them with this artwork in Iceland, Ono unites hopes for a better future from people everywhere.

When the lights are *on*, the monument transforms completely. Powerful beams of light shoot straight up into the night sky, forming a glowing pillar of light that can be seen for kilometres. The ray of light symbolises hope, unity and the wish for world peace. The idea behind the work comes from Yoko Ono's lifelong commitment to peace, shared with her late husband John Lennon. The tower is meant to keep their message alive and inspire everyone to imagine – and work towards – a peaceful world.

The lights only shine on specific dates: from John Lennon's birthday (9 October) until 31 December, concluding with the New Year. This limited schedule is meant to keep its lighting meaningful and sustainable. If you plan to visit, check the dates in advance so you don't miss seeing the tower fully illuminated.

ABOUT YOKO ONO

Yoko Ono was born in 1933 in Tokyo, Japan. She is an artist, musician and peace activist known for her experimental and poetic work. Her art often deals with themes like peace, love and connection. She invites people to take part in her work, encouraging them to think about their role in the world. While Ono is perhaps best known for her collaborations with John Lennon, her creative voice is powerful and unmistakably her own.

Wish Tree

Become part of Yoko Ono's art

- **Wish Tree for Washington, DC, AT THE HIRSHHORN MUSEUM, WASHINGTON, DC, USA**

  Tie your hopes and dreams to a *Wish Tree* in Washington, DC (USA) at the Hirshhorn Museum. Yoko Ono's interactive artwork invites visitors to write a wish on a slip of paper and attach it to the branches of a living tree. Over time, the tree becomes covered with countless messages, each one a glimpse into someone's private hope or dream. Together they form a powerful reminder of our shared desires.

- **SEND A POSTCARD OR AN EMAIL**

  Not able to visit the *Wish Tree*? You can also send your wishes via email or postcard:
  wish@imaginepeacetower.com
  IMAGINE PEACE TOWER
  PO Box 1009
  121 Reykjavík
  Iceland

- **Play It By Trust AT LONGHOUSE, EAST HAMPTON, USA**

  Interested in other artworks by Yoko Ono? Why not visit LongHouse in East Hampton, New York, and discover her work *Play It By Trust*. This large white chess set looks familiar at first, but instead of the usual black and white pieces, the pieces are all white. Once you start to play, you realise it's impossible to tell the sides apart. The game transforms conflict into collaboration, emphasising trust and peace. Just as Ono's original 1966 instruction reads: 'For playing as long as you can remember where all your pieces are'.

Play It By Trust

San Rocco

20.

Zhang Enli

A Cheerful Person

Montabone, Italy

In the hills of Montabone, a small village in Italy's Piemonte region, Zhang Enli transformed the façade of the 18th-century Church of San Rocco into the artwork *A Cheerful Person*. The work was unveiled in 2022 as part of Art Mapping Piemonte, a project that connects contemporary artists with rural locations. Instead of treating the church as a backdrop, Enli turned its very architecture into his canvas.

Approaching the church along the winding road, the painted façade stands out like a friendly landmark. At first glance, the 'face' seems simplistic, almost cartoonish. Using broad, gestural brushstrokes in greens, reds and ochres – colours that echo the vineyards and landscape around Montabone – Enli animated the building's surface. The rose window, arched doorway and decorative details are reimagined as facial features. As you move closer, the image breaks down into brushwork and colour and then transforms again as you step back. This shifting perception is central to the experience. The small church becomes animated, not through technology or spectacle, but through paint and imagination. From a distance, the church seems to smile. Up close, the face dissolves into sweeping lines and patches of colour that follow the contours of the stone.

Enli conceived of the project during the pandemic years and intended the painting to create a sense of joy and to offer visitors a fleeting smile. It also connects to a wider tradition of artists reimagining rural chapels in Piemonte, such as the celebrated Barolo Chapel. But while that earlier project relied on bold geometry (the signature style of its creators Sol LeWitt and David Tremlett), Enli emphasises spontaneity, using marks that resemble doodles or improvised sketches. The effect is deliberately playful, a reminder of the power of simple gestures to transform mood.

ABOUT ZHANG ENLI

Zhang Enli was born in 1965 in Jilin, China. The artist is recognised for his paintings and large-scale wall works. He often takes inspiration from everyday surroundings, using them as starting points for broader reflections on space and perception. He is inspired by daily life, memory and the relationship between people and their environments. Zhang's style is marked by fluid brushstrokes, subdued but distinctive colours and a direct, accessible approach that gives the ordinary a new presence.

Three tips for art churches in Piemonte

- **SOL LEWITT AND DAVID TREMLETT, BAROLO CHAPEL, LA MORRA**
  High above the vineyards of La Morra stands the Barolo Chapel, a tiny former farm shelter transformed in 1999 by Sol LeWitt and David Tremlett. LeWitt covered the exterior with vivid blocks of colour, while Tremlett created soft pastel interiors. Together, they transformed a crumbling structure into one of Piemonte's most photographed landmarks. The chapel is best visited at the golden hour, when the colours glow against the vines.

- **OLIVIER MOSSET, Griglie d'oro, NOVELLO**
  In the village of Novello, Swiss artist Olivier Mosset gave new life to a Brutalist water tower. His permanent installation, *Griglie d'oro (Golden grids)*, adds gleaming details: a golden roof, gate and metal grilles. The contrast of raw concrete and gold emphasises the essential value of water in this wine-growing region. Easily accessible on foot, it is the newest addition to Piemonte's growing collection of contemporary art in rural settings.

- **DAVID TREMLETT, CHURCH OF BEATA MARIA VERGINE DEL CARMINE, COAZZOLO**
  Not far from Asti, in the village of Coazzolo, British artist David Tremlett has completely painted the Church of Beata Maria Vergine del Carmine. Using his signature pastel pigments, he covered the exterior in large geometric fields of terracotta, ochre and earthy green – colours that echo the surrounding hills. Tremlett had previously collaborated with Sol LeWitt on the famous Barolo Chapel; in Coazzolo, he carries the dialogue between art, nature and spirituality forward on his own.

Piemonte

The Americas

21.

Ai Weiwei
Iron Tree

Frederik Meijer Gardens & Sculpture Park,
Grand Rapids, Michigan, USA

In the middle of the Frederik Meijer Gardens & Sculpture Park in Michigan stands *Iron Tree*, a striking work by Chinese artist Ai Weiwei. Nearly seven metres tall, the sculpture immediately catches the eye with its unusual mix of natural shape and industrial detail. From a distance, it resembles a dead tree – gnarled, bare and weathered by time. But as you come closer, it becomes clear this is no tree at all. The surface is iron, not bark. The branches are not grown but cast in sections. Heavy bolts, seams and joints are all clearly visible.

The sculpture is built from 99 separate iron pieces, each cast to look like real wood and then assembled into a single tree. It makes no attempt to appear natural. Instead, it clearly reveals its construction. The tree, made of heavy metal instead of living wood, feels both ancient and manufactured. Placed within the natural landscape of the sculpture park, the work interacts with the real trees around it. It changes with the seasons and the light. In autumn, its rust tones echo the falling leaves. In winter, it stands stark against the snow.

Ai Weiwei often uses form and material to reflect on identity, memory and tradition. *Iron Tree* expresses these ideas through its form: in Chinese culture, trees stand for growth, renewal and the connection between earth and sky. Here, that symbol is reimagined. There is also a social message. The tree can be seen as a symbol of community, made up of many individuals joined together. Though each part is different from the others, they depend on one another to create something whole.

ABOUT AI WEIWEI

Ai Weiwei was born in 1957 in Beijing, China. He takes inspiration from Chinese culture, history and politics. His work often uses traditional materials like wood, metal or porcelain to ask big questions about freedom, truth and power. He mixes craftsmanship with conceptual art to show how the past and present connect. His art, which is both personal and political, always aims to make people reflect and look more closely at the world around them.

Three other must-see artworks in Frederik Meijer Gardens & Sculpture Park

- **LOUISE NEVELSON, Atmosphere and Environment XI**
  This black steel sculpture consists of stacked geometric shapes that form a screen-like structure. Its sharp lines and deep shadows create a strong visual rhythm. Nevelson's signature use of assemblage, monochrome colour and architectural form transforms ordinary shapes into abstract environments.

- **ZHANG HUAN, Long Island Buddha**
  Set beside a quiet pond, this large copper Buddha head rests peacefully in the Japanese garden. With closed eyes and a calm face, it radiates silence. The sculpture blends Buddhist symbolism with modernist scale, offering a space for thought.

- **GIUSEPPE PENONE, It Will Continue to Grow Except at That Point**
  This poetic work features a bronze hand that gently holds a living tree. The tree keeps growing, except at the point where it is touched. The sculpture explores the meeting of nature and human gesture. It shows how we shape the world, and how it shapes us.

Zhang Huan, Long Island Buddha

PRADA
MARFA
PRADA
MARFA
PRADA
PRADA

22.

Elmgreen & Dragset

Prada Marfa

Marfa, Texas, USA

About 42 kilometres northwest of the tiny West Texas town of Marfa (population under 2,000), a curious sight appears on the roadside of U.S. Route 90: a Prada store standing alone under the wide Texas sky. It seems like a mirage, an impossibly out-of-place luxury boutique amid the dust, yucca and desert grasses of the Chihuahuan Desert.

A closer look reveals that it isn't a functioning store after all: the door does not open, and all that is visible through the two shop windows are 14 right-footed Prada shoes and 6 handbags. The artist duo responsible for this work, Elmgreen & Dragset, described it as a 'pop architectural land art project': a whimsical, sculptural intervention that invites viewers to reflect on consumerism, the luxury goods industry and gentrification. Fun fact: the items at the store are from the 2005 fall/winter Prada collection, handpicked by Miuccia Prada, who, contrary to popular belief, had nothing to do with the conception of the project.

The artists found inspiration in the words of the Danish poet Inger Christensen: 'A desert can be so desolate that nobody knows it exists.' Constructed from adobe bricks, plaster, paint, glass panes, aluminium framing, MDF and carpet, the original intention was for the structure to be left to slowly decay, overtaken by the natural elements. However, on the night of its completion, vandals graffitied the storefront and broke in to steal its contents, prompting a shift in plans. After being restored, the installation has been meticulously maintained by a local artist and protected by a security system. Its brush with vandalism has only added to its lore, making it an even more iconic landmark in the West Texas desert.

ABOUT ELMGREEN & DRAGSET

Michael Elmgreen was born in 1961 in Copenhagen, Denmark, and his partner in crime, Ingar Dragset, was born in 1969 in Trondheim, Norway. They have worked together as an artist duo since 1995, after meeting in a nightclub in Copenhagen. In their work, Elmgreen & Dragset critically examine cultural and political frameworks, delving into how identity and belonging are shaped within society. They are intrigued by the ways conversations shift when everyday objects are placed in unexpected contexts and when traditional ways of displaying art are challenged.

'A desert can be so desolate that nobody knows it exists.'

Danish poet Inger Christensen, who inspired Elmgreen & Dragset

Three must-see sites in Marfa

- **THE CHINATI FOUNDATION**
  In the late 1960s, artist Donald Judd sought an open, remote place, away from the limitations of the New York City art scene. He found it in Marfa, a High Desert town where he gradually acquired 22 buildings and the nearly 140-hectare Fort D.A. Russell. Judd transformed these spaces into a unique ecosystem for art, inviting artists like Roni Horn and Richard Long to create site-specific installations. In 1986, he established The Chinati Foundation to preserve and present large-scale, permanent works, including his own.

- **BUILDING 98**
  On the grounds of The Chinati Foundation sits Building 98, a historical site and art centre that blends contemporary art with military history. It is home to the famous World War II prisoner-of-war murals by Hans Jürgen Press and Robert Humpel.

- **BALLROOM MARFA**
  Ballroom Marfa is a renowned contemporary art space housed in a 1920s-era ballroom, offering artists and musicians a rare opportunity to engage with the vast Big Bend landscape.

Desert landscape in Marfa

23.

Hélio Oiticica,
Invenção da cor, Penetrável Magic Square #5, De Luxe

Inhotim, Brumadinho, Brazil

Inhotim is a vast open-air museum and botanical garden in Brumadinho, Brazil, where contemporary art is exhibited across lush tropical landscapes. Exploring Inhotim properly takes time. It's worth setting aside at least two days to see everything it has to offer. As you move along paths surrounded by dense greenery, ponds and carefully maintained gardens, you will encounter artworks and pavilions placed throughout this tropical setting, making nature an integral part of how the art is experienced.

Within this lush natural environment you'll find *Invenção da cor, Penetrável Magic Square #5, De Luxe (Invention of colour: Penetrable Magic Square #5, De Luxe)* by Brazilian modernist artist Hélio Oiticica. It is an outdoor installation made from tall concrete walls painted in vivid red, yellow, blue and white. Arranged in a square grid, the walls create open corridors you can walk through. The ground is covered with rounded stones, so you feel the texture of the ground under your feet. The piece starkly stands out against the surrounding plants and water, the bright colours and rigid lines contrasting with its lush green surroundings.

This work is meant to be entered and explored. Instead of just looking at it, visitors walk inside and choose their own path through it. Oiticica's idea was to create spaces people could experience directly and physically, instead of from a distance. Inhotim's natural setting supports this goal, making the work feel open and accessible.

Inhotim, Brazil

ABOUT HÉLIO OITICICA

Hélio Oiticica was born in 1937 in Rio de Janeiro, Brazil, and passed away in 1980. He is known for his bold use of colour and immersive, participatory environments. Inspired by Rio's street culture and the vibrancy of Brazilian life, he developed a radical visual language of geometric forms and walk-in structures. His work explores themes of freedom, social inclusion and the blurring of art and daily experience.

'Colour is the first revelation of the world.'

Hélio Oiticica

Three tips for other artworks in Inhotim

- **CHRIS BURDEN, Beehive Bunker**
  Installed on one of Inhotim's highest points, this military-like structure is made of stacked concrete bags that form a dome with openings, resembling a beehive. The work highlights themes of isolation, surveillance and the human urge to build protective and defensive spaces in elevated, strategic locations.

- **YAYOI KUSAMA, Narcissus Garden**
  In *Narcissus Garden* by Yayoi Kusama (p. 208), 750 stainless steel spheres float on a reflecting pool, echoing the myth of Narcissus. The balls mirror viewers, water and plants, with wind shifting them into new patterns. They create shimmering, ever-changing compositions that playfully reflect on the notion of vanity.

- **OLAFUR ELIASSON, Viewing Machine, 2001/2008**
  Visitors can rotate this large, hexagonal kaleidoscope by Olafur Eliasson (p. 80) and aim it in any direction. As the kaleidoscope moves, its inner mirrors create layered, fragmented reflections of the landscape. By controlling its angle, viewers reshape their surroundings into abstract, shifting patterns.

Olafur Eliasson, Viewing Machine

Yayoi Kusama, Narcissus Garden

24.

Hugh Hayden
Huff and a Puff

deCordova Sculpture Park and Museum,
Lincoln, Massachusetts, USA

At deCordova Sculpture Park and Museum in Massachusetts, Hugh Hayden's *Huff and a Puff* immediately catches the eye. The work is a full-scale replica of Henry David Thoreau's cabin at Walden Pond, tilted both forwards and sideways as if pushed off balance. With its wood shingles, custom bricks and mirrored windows, the structure looks familiar yet strangely unstable. The mirrors reflect the visitor and the surrounding landscape, merging past and present, myth and reality.

Thoreau, the 19th-century writer and philosopher, built his modest cabin at Walden Pond to live a simple life and to study the natural world, an experiment he described in his influential book *Walden*. His retreat has since become a symbol of independence and harmony with nature. Hayden takes this icon – long celebrated in American culture – and reshapes it to expose the tension beneath that ideal. The dramatic lean of the building suggests fragility and pressure, hinting at issues such as the economic realities of homeownership, unequal access to 'simplicity' and retreat, and the environmental strains that confront contemporary life.

The experience of approaching *Huff and a Puff* is both playful and unsettling. The crooked angles distort your sense of space, and the mirrored panes draw you in, layering your reflection over the cabin's façade. What seems at first like a nostalgic gesture towards a simpler time instead becomes an invitation to reconsider those ideals in today's world. Hayden transforms an American cultural icon into a work that asks us to reflect on how myths of freedom and self-sufficiency fit into current realities of inequality and environmental change.

ABOUT HUGH HAYDEN

Hugh Hayden was born in 1983 in Dallas, USA. His work transforms familiar forms into unsettling hybrids. Drawing inspiration from cultural myths, history and everyday objects, he explores themes of identity, social tension and belonging. Trained as an architect, Hayden often manipulates domestic or iconic structures – adding branches, distortions or shifts in scale – to question ideas of home, heritage and the American Dream.

deCordova Sculpture Park

Three other remarkable artworks disguised as houses

- **DO HO SUH, Fallen Star, SAN DIEGO**
  Perched askew University of California San Diego's Jacobs School of Engineering building, Do Ho Suh's *Fallen Star* resembles a blue cottage that has landed mid-gust. A small rooftop garden guides you to the skewed front door. Inside, floors and walls tilt, creating a playful sense of vertigo as homely details make the scene feel familiar and uncanny at the same time. The work reflects Suh's themes of home, migration and memory, while framing surprising views over the campus and the Torrey Pines plateau.

- **ERWIN WURM, Narrow House, LE HAVRE**
  Narrow House in Le Havre, France, is a permanently sited, life-sized reconstruction of Wurm's 1960s childhood home – compressed to uncanny proportions. Set within a landscaped, tree-lined square that evokes a suburban garden, the work reads like a familiar house seen through a funhouse mirror: doors, windows and roof all appear plausibly real yet unsettlingly thin, sharpening your sense of scale and perspective in the open air.

- **RACHEL WHITEREAD, Shack I AND Shack II, JOSHUA TREE NATIONAL PARK**
  Two quiet, concrete casts of former desert cabins sit in the High Desert landscape just outside Joshua Tree National Park (USA). Whiteread poured concrete into the existing structures and removed the outer shells, leaving solid, windowless 'fossils' of lived space. Their pale surfaces echo sand and scrub; their silence invites slow looking. Circling the shacks, you notice textures, seams and the residue of past lives turning absence into a tangible presence against the wide sky.

Do Ho Suh, Fallen Star

25.

James Turrell
Unseen Blue

James Turrell Museum, Molinos, Argentina

Swiss-born entrepreneur and collector Donald Hess first arrived in northern Argentina in the late 1990s, searching for vineyards that matched his ambition to develop wines under extreme conditions. After exploring Chile and the Argentinian region of Mendoza, he travelled further north and discovered the vineyard El Arenal, a site 2,600 metres above sea level, as well as the historic Colomé estate, which has been producing wine since 1831. These vineyards – among the highest in the world – became the foundation for his concept of 'high-altitude wines', crafted in limited quantities and under sustainable practices.

At Colomé, you will also find the James Turrell Museum, the only institution dedicated exclusively to this light artist. The museum sits at 2,300 metres and presents nine permanent works representing four decades of Turrell's career. At its heart is *Unseen Blue*, the largest skyspace the artist has built. Turrell's skyspaces can be found all over the world and consist of an enclosed square room or space with a partly open roof that frames the sky as if it were a canvas. Changing light – for instance at sunrise and sunset – transforms your perception of colour and depth: it is a type of work that is best experienced for longer periods of time as well as during different times of the day.

Surrounding this centrepiece are eight additional light installations, together with works on paper that trace Turrell's exploration of perception. Turrell himself worked closely on the design of these spaces, noting that Colomé's altitude, brilliant skies and isolation make it uniquely suited to his practice. He has described the site as a place where the intensity and clarity of the light give his work a power found nowhere else.

ABOUT JAMES TURRELL

James Turrell was born in 1943 in Los Angeles, USA. Influenced by his Quaker upbringing and trained in psychology and art, he emerged in the 1960s as a leading figure of California's Light and Space movement, which explored perception through light, colour and spatial experience rather than traditional materials. Working with natural and artificial light, Turrell creates environments that heighten perception and invite contemplation. Since the late 1970s, he has been developing his most ambitious project, Roden Crater – a dormant volcano in Arizona transformed into an observatory where visitors will (eventually) experience celestial events through his installations.

The Colomé estate

Three other spectacular art destinations in Latin America

- **MUSEO FRIDA KAHLO, MEXICO CITY**
  Visit Casa Azul in Coyoacán, Mexico City, the house where Frida Kahlo was born, lived with Diego Rivera and welcomed famous people, ranging from Russian revolutionary Leon Trotsky to surrealist artist André Breton. Since 1958 it has been a museum, displaying her art, personal belongings and the vibrant environment that shaped her creativity. A new space – Casa Roja – has opened next door as an extension of this cultural landmark, highlighting Kahlo's early life, family and private world.

- **MUSEUM OF ANTIOQUIA, MEDELLÍN**
  The Museum of Antioquia in Medellín (Colombia) is a must-see stop for fans of Colombian artist Fernando Botero, who donated many of his privately held works to the museum collection. Visitors can explore Botero's iconic 'Boterismo' style – voluminous figures that mix satire, politics and humour. Just outside, Plaza Botero extends the experience into the public space, with more than 20 of his monumental bronze sculptures on display.

- **CULIACÁN BOTANICAL GARDEN, CULIACÁN**
  The Culiacán Botanical Garden in Mexico, set amid lush tropical flora, integrates into its landscape large-scale installations and sculptures by international artists, such as the Argentine artist Adrián Villar Rojas and Brazilian artist Valeska Soares. Don't miss the work *Game Over* by Mexican artist Francis Alÿs, featuring a real, crashed 1993 Volkswagen Beetle, ploughed into the trunk of a large parota tree. It is deliberately left there to rust and be overtaken by plants and insects. But this dramatic sculptural remnant is only part of the work: be sure to watch the short film *Vocho,* which documents the entire performative act that produced it.

Museo Frida Kahlo

26.

Maya Lin
Storm King Wavefield

Storm King Art Center, New Windsor, New York, USA

An artwork made not of oil paint or bronze, but of earth and grass: Maya Lin's 4.5-hectare *Storm King Wavefield* invites you to walk, run or even roll on its gentle curves. Bringing the sense of an ocean to New York State's Hudson Valley, the waves of earth and grass encourage you to engage with the piece, inviting you to be playful while grounding you at the same time.

To get a sense of its scale, imagine: the seven waves stretch nearly 122 metres in length and rise about 3 to 4.5 metres high – comparable to the size of mid-ocean waves. With its use of organic materials, the *Storm King Wavefield* is a living, evolving artwork – an artwork natural and illogical at the same time, designed to help you lose yourself in every sense of the word.

But there is more to this artwork than meets the eye. Lin's art is concerned with our environment, and she uses her artwork to draw our attention back to the land itself. *Storm King Wavefield*, surrounded by the Schunnemunk Mountain and the Hudson Highlands, is created on reclaimed gravel pits, reminding us of the damage we leave behind, but also of how land can heal if we choose to take action. By shaping the earth into something that feels both natural and carefully held, Lin invites us to consider our place within the landscape and the responsibility we have to protect it.

Lin's *Storm King Wavefield* is the largest wavefield she has created: the other two can be found in Ann Arbor, Michigan, and Miami, Florida.

ABOUT MAYA LIN

Maya Lin was born in 1959 in Athens (Ohio), USA. She is known for her sculptural works as well as historical memorials, such as the Vietnam Veterans Memorial in Washington, DC, which she designed after winning a competition when she was only an undergraduate architecture student at Yale University. Lin draws inspiration from nature, Japanese and Native American culture, and works by American land artists of the 1960s and ’70s, making her mark in the traditionally male-dominated field of Land Art with her signature minimalist, poetic interventions.

‘If any art form, anything, gets us to take a moment's pause and look at something afresh, that's got to be a good thing.’

Maya Lin

Other things to see at Storm King Art Center

- **MARTIN PURYEAR, Lookout**
  Also on view at the 200-hectare outdoor museum Storm King Art Center, amongst over 100 large scale sculptures and site-specific works, is Martin Puryear's (p. 70) *Lookout*. Step inside this curved shape made out of brick, referencing the industrial history of the area and featuring 90 oculi (round openings) that look out over the trees and sky.

- **ALEXANDER CALDER, The Arch**
  Upon entering Storm King on foot, you are greeted by the iconic *The Arch*, a large sculpture by Alexander Calder. Monumental yet elegant, the matte-black steel work stands in stark contrast to the lush green landscape.

- **ALICJA KWADE, LinienLand**
  Don't miss Alicja Kwade's (p. 18) artwork *LinienLand*, a gravity-defying steel structure with natural stone spheres, sourced from various continents.

Alicja Kwade, LinienLand

27.

Pascale Marthine Tayou

Mikado Tree

Donum Estate, Sonoma, California, USA

Upon first encountering this sculpture by Pascale Marthine Tayou, set amid the lush vineyards of the Donum Estate, your first reaction may be one of frustration. Perhaps it recalls childhood games of Mikado (pick-up sticks) and the endless disputes with siblings over whether a stick had actually moved or not – a game less about winning than it is about cheating and arguing. This memory seems to align with the artist's intent: Tayou uses the form of Mikado sticks to suggest both playfulness and danger. For him, the game is a metaphor for the complexity of the world, and how navigating it can be as attractive as it can be risky.

Mikado Tree feels both in and out of place amid the endless rows of grape vines. It blends with the few scattered trees, yet it is immediately recognisable as man-made: a tall sculpture of aluminium and concrete. From a distance, it resembles a perfectly manicured tree – or even a flower, like a dandelion gone to seed, waiting for a child to blow on it and make a wish. Up close, however, it turns gnarly: its sharp sticks jut outwards as if to warn you to keep your distance.

The game of Mikado has an intriguing history: it was first mentioned in Buddhist writings of the fifth century AD, after which it spread across Asia to Europe and eventually to the Americas. For Tayou, the game embodies a universality of human experience, captured in his words: 'There are no borders in culture.'

ABOUT PASCALE MARTHINE TAYOU

Pascale Marthine Tayou was born in Nkongsamba, Cameroon, in 1966. Originally educated in law, he developed his artistic practice without formal training. He lived around the world before settling in Belgium. Working in sculpture, installation, drawing and video, his art often reflects his own presence and identity, while also engaging with questions of movement, cultural exchange and the interconnected world ('global village').

Yayoi Kusama, Pumpkin

Three other works to see at the Donum Estate

- **ZHAN WANG, Artificial Rock No. 126**

  The Donum Collection spans over 80 hectares (almost a square kilometre) and features over 60 artworks, many of them monumental outdoor sculptures by a wide range of international artists. Among the first works installed at the Donum Estate is Zhan Wang's *Artificial Rock No. 126*. This work is inspired by traditional Chinese scholars' rocks, which are naturally eroded stones used for contemplation. The artist recreates their organic forms in hand-forged polished stainless steel, transforming them into a giant mirror-like sculpture that reflects the surrounding vineyards and the sky. With this work, Zhan Wang seamlessly fuses ancient tradition with contemporary materiality.

- **AI WEIWEI, Circle of Animals/Zodiac Heads**

  Ai Weiwei's bronze *Circle of Animals/Zodiac Heads*, part of the Donum Collection, reimagines the 12 animal figures that once decorated Beijing's Yuanmingyuan palace before being looted by French and British forces in 1860. Through this work, the artist (p. 120) raises questions about cultural heritage, ownership and memory, while also inviting a personal connection – after all, everyone has a zodiac sign. Feeling inspired and thirsty? Weiwei created a special series of Donum wine labels inspired by the animals in this sculpture, with each vintage paired to the animal sign of its year.

- **YAYOI KUSAMA, Pumpkin**

  On the estate, you will also encounter one of Yayoi Kusama's iconic pumpkins. In Japan during World War II, when food was scarce and hunger shaped daily life, Kusama (p. 208) was lucky to grow up surrounded by pumpkins from her family's business. The abundance of this humble vegetable left a deep imprint on her imagination. What began as nourishment soon became inspiration: her earliest painting was of a pumpkin, and the form has remained a central motif in her work for more than 70 years.

Zhan Wang, Artificial Rock No.126

28.

Simone Leigh
Satellite

Glenstone, Potomac, Maryland, USA

Standing almost 7.5 metres tall, this towering bronze figure of a woman carries a layered history with her. Her body is modelled after the D'mba, a sculptural form created by the Baga people of West Africa and used in ancestral rituals – a tradition later appropriated by Western artists like Pablo Picasso. Her head is shaped like a Zulu ceremonial spoon but also resembles the form of a satellite dish. She becomes both receiver and transmitter: a conduit of signals, stories and knowledge. Her face, however, remains abstract and featureless. Her eyelessness becomes both a form of resistance and a shield: it denies others the return of her gaze, while concealing her inner self from being fully seen – or consumed.

Her breasts emphasise the female body, evoking associations with maternity, fertility, sexuality and labour. By bringing these parts together – the nourishing body and the dish-shaped head – Leigh honours the labour and care of Black women, both physical and emotional – care that, while sustaining life and carrying memory, has too often gone unrecognised.

Clay is foundational to Leigh's practice: most of her bronze sculptures are first modelled in clay. This choice of material holds meaning for Leigh, representing women's labour in domestic crafts and decoration – a form of art often underappreciated throughout (art) history. By transforming clay into monumental bronze sculptures, Leigh elevates these forms of care and labour into enduring symbols, demanding recognition and respect.

ABOUT SIMONE LEIGH

Simone Leigh was born in 1967 in Chicago, USA. She is known for her sculptures, though she also creates works involving video, installation and social practice (collaborative, community-engaged, socially conscious art). In her practice, Leigh consistently centres the female body – particularly the Black female body – as a site of power, care and resilience.

Felix Gonzalez-Torres, "Untitled"

Other must-see artworks at Glenstone

- **JEFF KOONS, Split-Rocker**
  There are many other worthwhile works in the sculpture garden at Glenstone, a private museum of contemporary art just outside of Washington, DC. Combining art and nature is Jeff Koons (p. 44) with his sculpture *Split-Rocker*: a giant over 11 metres tall, whose playful head is split into two halves, modelled after a toy pony rocker and a toy dinosaur rocker, covered in a blanket of live flowers that bloom seasonally.

- **FELIX GONZALEZ-TORRES, "Untitled"**
  Felix Gonzalez-Torres's "Untitled" installation at Glenstone consists of two shallow, marble, circular pools of water: a work inviting reflection – both literal and emotional. As is common in Gonzalez-Torres's work, the piece explores themes of presence and absence, love and loss, and the passage of time.

- **ROBERT GOBER, Two Partially Buried Sinks**
  Robert Gober, much like Felix Gonzalez-Torres, was heavily influenced by the tragedy of the AIDS epidemic in the 1980s. At Glenstone, he handcrafts two objects in the shape of sinks as a poetic symbol to challenge the misconception that AIDS results from poor hygiene – the two sinks are positioned to resemble two tomb stones.

Robert Gober, Two Partially Buried Sinks

Jeff Koons, Split-Rocker

29.

Susan Philipsz
We'll All Go Together

Powder Art Foundation, Eden, Utah, USA

High on the slopes of Powder Mountain in Utah, Susan Philipsz's sound piece *We'll All Go Together* turns a winter landscape into an unexpected listening space. Installed along a tree-lined ski run, the work uses hidden speakers to play the artist's own untrained, unaccompanied voice singing an old American hymn in canon. Skiers passing by may catch the first strains of her voice almost by accident – just a phrase drifting in the cold air – before realising they are encountering an artwork.

The idea behind the work is both simple and profound. Philipsz deliberately uses her unpolished, personal singing rather than a formal, polished recording. Each vocal line follows the next in canon, creating a layered, echoing effect that evokes the cyclical nature of life and death. By placing this meditative music in the middle of a recreational ski area, Philipsz reframes what it means to move through the landscape: the mountain is no longer just for speed and sport, but also for contemplation and reflection.

The sound is gentle and sometimes elusive, merging with natural noises like wind in the trees or the soft scrape of skis on snow. The silence between phrases becomes part of the composition, providing space for thought. Rather than commanding attention, the work offers a quiet invitation to pause and appreciate the delicate beauty of the world around us.

The piece is part of the Powder Art Foundation's vision to weave contemporary art into the mountain landscape. By commissioning site-specific installations, the foundation enriches Powder Mountain beyond its traditional use for skiing, creating a space where art and nature meet.

ABOUT SUSAN PHILIPSZ

Susan Philipsz was born in 1965 in Glasgow, Scotland. She is known for her powerful sound installations that take inspiration from folk-songs and classical music. Philipsz uses her own untrained voice to create works that fill public spaces with emotion. Her art is simple but moving, turning places like bridges or forests into spaces for quiet listening and reflection.

'I am particularly interested in the emotive and psychological properties of sound and how it can be used as a device to alter individual consciousness.'

Susan Philipsz

Three other artworks to see on Powder Mountain

- **GERARD & KELLY, Relay (Powder Mountain)**
  The artist duo redesigned a covered ski lift at Powder Mountain by adding bright vinyl strips to its canopy. These coloured bands create bold, shifting patterns as the light changes during the day. Skiers riding up pass through a vivid tunnel of colour that turns an ordinary lift ride into a striking visual experience.

- **DAVINA SEMO, Listener, Reflector, Mother**
  Three large bronze bells titled *Listener, Reflector,* and *Mother* are installed in different spots on Powder Mountain. Made with warm-toned, perforated surfaces, they catch light in interesting ways. Visitors can ring them, producing deep, resonant sounds that add an interactive and striking feature to the mountain landscape.

- **GRIFFIN LOOP, Launch Intention**
  A large steel sculpture shaped like a paper aeroplane sits on a wooded trail at Powder Mountain. As hikers and bikers pass underneath it, its smooth, angled design suggests motion and flight, adding a dramatic, eye-catching element to the path and turning a simple trail into a memorable landmark.

Gerard & Kelly, Relay (Powder Mountain)

Griffin Loop, Launch Intention

30.

Ugo Rondinone
Seven Magic Mountains

Henderson, Nevada, USA

As you drive out of Las Vegas into a vast stretch of untouched nature, it is hard to comprehend how this glitzy city seems to have just been dropped into the rugged desert. About 32 kilometres outside Las Vegas, as you approach *Seven Magic Mountains*, the contrast between nature and artifice becomes more pronounced. Rising from the Mojave Desert like otherworldly guardians, Ugo Rondinone's towering, neon totem-like structures punctuate the landscape with a burst of form and colour.

At first glance, they resemble rock stacks or cairns – those little stone markers found on trails across the world. However, Rondinone took inspiration from so-called hoodoos: tall, weather-sculpted spires found in many national parks throughout the American Southwest.

Standing around 10 metres tall, each of these gravity-defying stacks is composed of massive, locally sourced boulders – 33 in total – held together by a steel backbone. Each stone, weighing between 9,100 and 22,700 kilograms, is carefully balanced in a stack ranging from three to six stones high, standing against the gorgeous backdrop of Jean Dry Lake and the McCullough Range. Their surfaces, coated in two layers of vibrant fluorescent paint, are activated by the relentless desert sun, radiating an intensity that feels almost supernatural or even magical.

What makes Rondinone's work so compelling is the way that *Seven Magic Mountains* seems both ancient and modern at once. The blend of raw natural elements with bursts of bright colour, together with its symbolic shape, connects the work to traditions of storytelling and rituals.

ABOUT UGO RONDINONE

Ugo Rondinone was born in 1964 in Brunnen, Switzerland. He is known for his bold and playful works that explore the connection between art, nature and human emotion. Rondinone draws inspiration from history, pop culture and personal memories. You can find other outdoor works from Rondinone's *Mountain* series in Medellín (Colombia), Ermatingen (Switzerland), Miami (USA), Liverpool (UK) and Doha (Qatar). His artistic practice extends beyond these sculptures and includes paintings, installations and video works, often using symbolic imagery such as totems, masks, clouds and rainbows.

Other art sites to visit in Nevada

- **MICHAEL HEIZER, City, GARDEN VALLEY**
  Visit another astounding piece of land art: Michael Heizer's *City*. At about two and a half kilometres long, *City* is considered to be the largest land artwork in the world. While it's intended to resemble a massive urban complex, the city that Heizer created looks nothing like current metropoles. It is instead meant to recall prehistoric ones, with gigantic abstract forms composed of sand, cement and other materials that emerge from the Nevada desert.

- **JEAN DRY LAKE**
  Seven Magic Mountains stands close to another significant land art site: Jean Dry Lake. In the 1960s, both Jean Tinguely and Michael Heizer created works here. Over the decades, wind, erosion, pollution, human activity (the lakebed is now mainly used for off-road sports) and shifting sand have caused these works to fade and disintegrate. Today, they have almost entirely disappeared. Due to its natural beauty and historic significance, it is still a site worth visiting.

- **DAMIEN HIRST, The Empathy Suite AT THE PALMS CASINO RESORT IN LAS VEGAS**
  Feel like splurging? Book *The Empathy Suite* at The Palms Casino Resort in Las Vegas, a one-of-a-kind space designed by British artist Damien Hirst. Spanning over 830 square metres, *The Empathy Suite* is a masterpiece in its own right, with artworks adorning every surface. The price? A whopping $100,000 a night.

The Las Vegas Strip

31.

Walter De Maria
The Lightning Field

Dia Art Foundation, West central, New Mexico, USA

The Lightning Field is a monumental land art installation located in a remote desert area of western New Mexico. It consists of 400 polished stainless steel poles arranged in a precise grid, measuring one mile by one kilometre. The poles are about six metres tall, carefully adjusted so that their tips form an even horizontal plane despite the uneven desert terrain.

Walter De Maria designed *The Lightning Field* to be experienced slowly and thoughtfully. It is a sculpture meant to be walked through as well as viewed, inviting visitors to spend extended periods of time in the landscape. A full experience does not depend solely on lightning strikes – although these can create an exciting spectacle – but on observing changing light and weather conditions that dramatically transform the appearance of the poles. Visitors are especially encouraged to explore the field during sunrise and sunset, when the light shifts most beautifully. To support this, Dia Art Foundation offers overnight visits with a reservation from May to October for those who wish to spend the night at the site.

The grid's precise mathematical order stands in striking contrast to the rugged, open desert. As the sun rises, sets or moves behind clouds, the polished poles catch and reflect light in subtle, shifting ways. De Maria aimed to create an artwork that cannot be fully captured in photographs, encouraging people to experience the scale of the work directly in the vastness and sublimity of nature.

ABOUT WALTER DE MARIA

Walter De Maria was born in 1935 in Albany (California), USA, and he passed away in 2013. The artist is known for his important role in the Land Art movement. Inspired by geometry, nature and vast landscapes, he created large-scale, site-specific works that invite people to reflect on time, space and their surroundings. His art is marked by precise structures and simple materials, encouraging slow, careful observation.

Works of Walter De Maria around the world

- **The Broken Kilometer, NEW YORK CITY**
  The Broken Kilometer is an installation of 500 polished brass rods laid out in precise rows in an indoor art space in New York's bustling Soho neighbourhood. Arranged mathematically to span a full kilometre when placed end to end, the installation turns simple industrial materials into a contemplative exploration of measurement, repetition and space.

- **The New York Earth Room, NEW YORK CITY**
  The New York Earth Room is a permanent indoor installation near *The Broken Kilometer*, right next to fancy retail shops. The work consists of nearly 200 cubic metres of earth spread across a gallery on the second floor. The dark, damp soil fills the space with a surprising natural element, making you think about the landscape and the difference between nature and the man-made environment it is situated in.

- **The Vertical Earth Kilometer, KASSEL**
  The Vertical Earth Kilometer is a one-kilometre-long solid brass rod drilled straight down into the ground in Kassel, Germany. Hidden from view, except for its top end on a stone plate, the work marks distance underground in a simple, direct way, playing with ideas of measurement and what can and cannot be seen.

The Broken Kilometer

Asia & Oceania

32.

Antony Gormley
Inside Australia

Lake Ballard, Menzies, Australia

At Lake Ballard in western Australia, you will find one of Antony Gormley's most striking artworks. The project is called *Inside Australia*, and it includes 51 metal sculptures spread out over a wide salt flat. Each figure is based on a scan of a real person from the nearby town of Menzies. The sculptures are made of dark metal and stand in quiet stillness under the open sky.

Lake Ballard itself is a silent, remote and almost haunting place. The salt crust is pale and dry for most of the year, cracking underfoot as you walk. Low hills surround the flat expanse, and the red desert soil meets the white lakebed in sharp contrast. It is both vast and strangely intimate.

When you walk across the flat white surface of the lake you come across these strange and thin human forms, one by one. Some are tall and stretched while others look more compact. They are all different, but clearly part of the same family. The distance between them makes each figure feel alone, yet somehow still connected to the others. Light and shadow change the way the sculptures look throughout the day. Early in the morning or late in the afternoon, their long shadows stretch across the ground, making the scene even more dramatic and eerie. The setting is dry and empty, but on the rare occasions when it rains, the 'lake' turns into a shallow mirror. The figures then seem to rise out of the water, adding another layer to the experience.

The artwork makes you think about how people belong to a place, even when it feels empty or remote. Because the figures are so minimal – they do not show faces or clothes but are simple outlines, like shadows in metal – you start to see them as representatives of all humankind, not just as the townspeople of Menzies.

ABOUT ANTONY GORMLEY

Antony Gormley was born in 1950 in London, UK. He is known for his exploration of the human body in relation to space and landscape. His works often feature minimal, abstracted human forms made from materials like metal or stone. Gormley uses his own body as a starting point and draws inspiration from Buddhist philosophy, archaeology and architecture. His art invites viewers to reflect on presence, absence and how we experience our surroundings through the body.

Exposure

Three other artworks by Antony Gormley

- **Another Place, LIVERPOOL**
  On Crosby Beach near Liverpool in the UK, an 'army' of 100 cast-iron figures stretches for almost three kilometres along the shore. Each life-sized sculpture, modelled on the artist's own body, gazes out to sea, gradually submerged and revealed again by the tides. Both intimate and monumental, *Another Place* reflects on migration, the passage of time, and our deep, ever-changing relationship with the sea.

- **Exposure, LELYSTAD**
  The country of the Netherlands, though small enough to cross in three hours, is home to more than 50 land art works. Among these works is Antony Gormley's *Exposure* in Lelystad, a monumental crouching figure made from over 18,000 steel rods and 14,000 bolts, modelled on the artist's own body. The sculpture seems to be sitting quietly, watching out over the water, yet carries a subtle warning: with rising sea levels, water will one day reach the giant's feet – and the land behind it.

- **Room, LONDON**
  The bedroom of this unique suite in the Beaumont Mayfair hotel in London occupies the interior of a giant sculpture by Antony Gormley, which dominates the entrance front of The Beaumont. The towering structure is clad in dark steel blocks, creating a dramatic exterior. Inside, the minimalist bedroom is a calm, contemplative space, designed to invite introspection and disconnection from the outside world.

33.

Daniel Libeskind
Outside Line

Uozu, Japan

In the quiet forests of Uozu stands *Outside Line*, an eye-catching installation by architect Daniel Libeskind. A vivid red steel beam cuts through the landscape in a jagged, angular gesture. Supported by slender columns, *Outside Line* traces an imaginary axis between the Uozu Buried Forest Museum – home to ancient, preserved trees – and the distant Tateyama Mountain Range. The bright red line hovers above a staircase, inviting visitors to walk beneath it and become part of its composition. Its sharp, flowing form suggests a heartbeat or the fluid lines of calligraphy, connecting the artwork to Japanese artistic traditions.

As the seasons change, the installation comes alive in new ways. Snow settles into its sharp angles in winter, highlighting its precise geometry. In the rainy season, water cascades along its surface, guiding the eye and footsteps upwards through the forest. This dynamic interplay of light, shadow and weather transforms *Outside Line* from a static sculpture into a living, ever-changing work.

Libeskind conceived the work as more than art: he shaped it as a meditative path encouraging reflection on time, memory and landscape. It embodies his philosophy of architecture as storytelling, using form to evoke meaning and emotion. By cutting straight through the landscape with a striking red line, *Outside Line* offers a spot-on example of how contemporary art and design can highlight connections between nature, history and location.

ABOUT DANIEL LIBESKIND

Daniel Libeskind was born in 1946 in Łódź, Poland. He is an architect known for bold, angular designs that evoke memory and emotion. Inspired by history, philosophy and music, his work often explores themes of loss and resilience. Libeskind's signature style features sharp lines, fractured forms and dramatic light, creating spaces that invite reflection. His approach blends art, design and architecture with storytelling.

Ryoji Ikeda, spectra

Three other artworks that cut boldly through earth, sky and water

- **MICHAEL HEIZER, Double Negative, MOAPA VALLEY**
  In the Nevada desert, Michael Heizer's *Double Negative* is a dramatic intervention in the earth. In 1969, two massive trenches, each stretching hundreds of metres long and almost 15 metres deep, were cut directly into the rocky plateau. The cuts face each other across a natural canyon, forming a monumental absence rather than a built object. By removing thousands of tons of rock, Heizer created a work that forces you to see the landscape through the void he carved into it.

- **RYOJI IKEDA, spectra, HOBART**
  At Mona (Museum of Old and New Art) in Hobart, Australia, Ryoji Ikeda's *spectra* sends 49 powerful beams of light high into the night sky. A great pillar of light reaching 15 kilometres into the darkness becomes visible for miles around. The work is usually switched on for the winter and summer solstices, marking these moments with an unforgettable glow. The lights are arranged in a precise grid, so that together they form a perfect square of light, giving the beam a sharp and architectural quality.

- **ROBERT SMITHSON, Broken Circle/Spiral Hill, EMMEN**
  In the Dutch town of Emmen, Robert Smithson created *Broken Circle/Spiral Hill,* one of his rare European land artworks. Situated in a former sand quarry, the piece joins two striking forms: a circular incision filled with water and an artificial hill topped with a spiralling path. By cutting directly into the earth, Smithson exposed geological layers and reshaped the site into a living sculpture. Visitors can walk along the spiral, climb the hill and experience the landscape as both artwork and terrain.

Ryoji Ikeda, Spectra

34.

Fujiko Nakaya
Khao Yai Fog Forest

Khao Yai Art Forest, Nakhon Ratchasima, Thailand

At Khao Yai Art Forest in Thailand, Fujiko Nakaya's *Khao Yai Fog Forest* transforms the hillside into a living artwork. Across the terrain, hidden nozzles release fine sprays of water vapour that rise and drift with the wind, clinging to trees or rolling across the grass in shifting waves. At times, the fog gathers in dense clouds; at others, it thins into a delicate veil. The work is never the same twice: it responds to temperature, light and humidity, making nature itself its co-creator.

Nakaya has worked with fog since the 1970s, and here she uses it to reveal both the beauty and fragility of the environment. The fog alternates between concealing and revealing the landscape, sharpening awareness of the surrounding forest while reminding us of the invisible systems – water, air, atmosphere – that sustain life. At Khao Yai, the installation also engages with sustainability: the mist is produced using renewable energy and water captured from the atmosphere, underlining a respectful partnership with nature rather than a spectacle imposed upon it.

Walking through *Khao Yai Fog Forest* is both physical and sensory. The scale is vast, stretching across the hillside, but the experience feels intimate. One moment you see the contours of the land, the next you are enveloped in white clouds: sounds muted, vision blurred. Your own presence – footsteps, breath, the sensation of moisture on skin – becomes part of the artwork. Rather than offering a fixed image, Nakaya's fog turns the forest into a shifting stage where nature performs in real time.

ABOUT FUJIKO NAKAYA

Fujiko Nakaya was born in 1933 in Sapporo, Japan. She is a pioneering artist renowned for her immersive fog sculptures, a form she has developed since the 1970s. Inspired by her father's scientific research into snow crystals, she brings art, science and natural phenomena together in works that explore the relationship between humans and the environment. Using fog as her primary medium, Nakaya creates ever-changing, site-specific installations that transform landscapes and architecture into atmospheric experiences.

'Fog makes visible things become invisible and invisible things – like wind – become visible.'

Fujiko Nakaya

Three other must-see artworks in Khao Yai Art Forest

- **UBATSAT, Pilgrimage to Eternity**
  For *Pilgrimage to Eternity*, Thai artist ubatsat installed 9 stupa (Buddhist monument) fragments throughout Khao Yai Art Forest. Made from local soil and placed directly on the ground, the pieces are left to be reclaimed by nature. Over time, they will erode and integrate into the landscape, reflecting Buddhist ideas of impermanence, renewal and the natural cycle of life and death.

- **ARAYA RASDJARMREARNSOOK, Two Planets Series**
  Araya Rasdjarmrearnsook's *Two Planets Series* situates video installations deep in the forest. In the films, groups of Thai villagers – farmers, workers, monks – react to reproductions of European masterpieces such as Édouard Manet's *The Luncheon on the Grass* or Jean-François Millet's *The Gleaners*. Their candid laughter and comments shift the viewer's role, provoking questions about perspective, knowledge and who is truly observing whom.

- **ELMGREEN & DRAGSET, K-BAR**
  K-BAR is a pavilion by Elmgreen & Dragset (p. 124) that doubles as a functioning bar. Open once a month, it pays homage to the late German artist Martin Kippenberger, whose painting *Untitled* (1996) forms the centrepiece, visible even when the bar is closed. Inside, visitors can enjoy a specially developed cocktail menu, while simultaneously savouring art, leisure and social encounters.

Araya Rasdjarmrearnsook, Two Planet Series

ubatsat, Pilgrimage to Eternity

35.

Louise Bourgeois
Maman

Ho-Am Art Museum, Yongin, South Korea

The Ho-Am Art Museum in Yongin, about an hour's journey outside the bustling city of Seoul, is part of the Samsung Foundation of Culture and opened in 1982 to present the collection of Samsung founder Lee Byung-chull, focusing on traditional Korean art. The museum is named after Byung-chull's nickname, Ho-Am. While the museum itself is definitely worth a visit, many visitors would agree that its 6.5-hectare traditional Korean garden, Hee Won, is the highlight.

As you enter through the traditional Bohwamun Gate, you pass a grove of plum trees before reaching the main garden with its ponds, pavilions, stone sculptures and a pagoda from the Goryeo period (a Korean dynasty that lasted between the 10th and 14th centuries AD). The site is also known for its seasonal appeal – especially its cherry blossoms in spring – and for the peacocks that roam the grounds.

The showstopper of the park is the monumental spider sculpture *Maman* by Louise Bourgeois, perched on the lake against a backdrop of mountains. For Bourgeois, the spider represents her mother ('maman' is French for 'mum'), who sadly passed away when Bourgeois was only 20 years old. Her mother worked as a tapestry restorer: the spider's labour of creating and fixing its web echoes her mother's weaving and mending. The sculpture's enormous size may make it seem intimidating – yet the space underneath its body also suggests shelter and protection. Bourgeois referred to her mother as her best friend, and said she was as 'deliberate, clever, patient, soothing, reasonable, dainty, subtle, indispensable, neat and useful as a spider'.

ABOUT LOUISE BOURGEOIS

Louise Bourgeois was born in Paris in 1911 and lived in New York City until her death in 2010. Across a career of more than 70 years, she worked in installation, drawing, printmaking and painting, though she is most renowned for her sculptural practice. Her art explores memory, love, fear and loss, transforming personal experiences into powerful artworks, ranging from monumental spiders to intimate fabric works and room-like installations.

'Every day you have to abandon your past or accept it, and then, if you cannot accept it, you become a sculptor.'

Louise Bourgeois

Three other stunning gardens around the world

- **KIRSTENBOSCH, CAPE TOWN**
  Kirstenbosch is a botanical garden on the eastern slopes of Table Mountain in Cape Town (South Africa), founded in 1913 as the first site in the world dedicated to preserving indigenous flora. It combines expansive outdoor landscapes with a large conservatory that showcases plants from ecological systems found in South Africa, such as fynbos (shrubland), savanna (grassland) and Karoo (semi-desert). The garden is especially renowned for its spectacular displays of proteas, including the king protea, South Africa's national flower. Kirstenbosch also integrates art into the setting, with regular displays of stone sculptures from Zimbabwean artists linked to the Chapungu Sculpture Park in Harare, Zimbabwe.

- **SINGAPORE BOTANIC GARDENS, SINGAPORE**
  Singapore Botanic Gardens is a tropical garden in the heart of Singapore, first established in 1859 and today recognised as a UNESCO World Heritage Site. Covering around 80 hectares (almost a square kilometre), it brings together themed landscapes and specialised collections, including the National Orchid Garden with over 1,000 species and 2,000 hybrids. The gardens are also home to sculptures and public artworks.

- **SALA KEOKU, NONG KHAI**
  Sala Keoku is a sculpture park near Nong Khai, Thailand, close to the Mekong River and the Laos border. Created from 1978 onwards by mystic and artist Luang Pu Bunleua Sulilat and his followers, the site – rich with trees, plants and a lively fish pond – features enormous concrete sculptures inspired by Buddhist and Hindu iconography, some rising to 25 metres high.

Kirstenbosch

Sala Keoku

36.

Richard Serra

East-West/West-East

Brouq Nature Reserve, Qatar

The exactness of the location of this artwork immediately makes you understand you are in for something unusual. *East-West/West-East* cannot be found on any map, nor are there any signs or even roads guiding you – all you have to go on are the GPS coordinates: N25° 31.019′ E050° 51.948′. Do not forget sun cream, water and plenty of petrol for the two-hour drive across the desert near the remote village of Zekreet. The vast stretch of sand is only disrupted by the occasional antelope or camel and – surprise – Film City, a structure once used for scenes in the Hollywood blockbuster movie *Transformers*. At last, you see Richard Serra's artwork emerging in the distance.

Is your mind playing tricks on you? Four enormous vertical steel plates, each around 14 metres high, stand in the desert landscape of the Brouq Nature Reserve. The plates are made from weathering (corten) steel, which creates a rust-like surface that blends with the natural landscape. The plates are placed in vertical alignment with each other, as well as in perfect harmony with the gypsum and limestone plateaus that have been carved over time by wind. The four pillars are placed across a distance of more than one kilometre, challenging your sense of perspective within the open flatness of the desert.

At first, it is hard to comprehend exactly what you are looking at. The tall plates seem otherworldly, as if they have always been there – remnants of an unknown civilisation. While exploring the site on foot, you will notice that the work shifts and changes with each step you take, disorienting you while revealing the desert's true scale and depth as you move around it. More than an artwork, it is a meditative experience that will stay with you.

ABOUT RICHARD SERRA

Richard Serra was born in 1938 in San Francisco, USA. His large-scale abstract sculptures, created for site-specific landscapes, cities and architectural settings, secured him international recognition as well as the title 'the poet of iron'. His work is associated with post-minimalism: an art movement that evolved from minimalism, using simple forms but adding texture, emotion and organic shapes to create a more expressive experience.

Museum of Islamic Art

Art sites worth a visit in Doha, Qatar

- **MUSEUM OF ISLAMIC ART**
  In front of the stunning Museum of Islamic Art (MIA), designed by I.M. Pei and a sight worth seeing in and of itself, you will find a second sculpture by Richard Serra. In this particular artwork, he pays homage to the number seven, a number of spiritual significance in Islamic culture, by incorporating seven weathered steel plates.

- **MONIRA AL QADIRI, Zephyr**
  Monira Al Qadiri's *Zephyr* consists of five glowing, plexiglass sculptures inspired by the microscopic marine organisms that produce nearly half the world's oxygen, reminding us of the Gulf's fragile ecosystems.

- **SHEZAD DAWOOD, Doha Modern Playground**
  In Al Masrah Park, Shezad Dawood turns six iconic Qatari modernist buildings, including the Sheraton Grand Doha Resort & Convention Hotel and Qatar National Theatre, into oversized slides, benches and climbing frames: part living archive, part playground.

Monira Al Qadiri, Zephyr

37.

Yayoi Kusama
Pumpkin

Benesse Art Site, Naoshima, Japan

On a narrow concrete pier that stretches into the calm Seto Inland Sea stands *Pumpkin* by Yayoi Kusama. Bright yellow with black polka dots, the sculpture is easy to spot. Its round shape and curled stem give it a cartoon-like appearance, but it also holds a quiet sense of weight. Surrounded by open sea, the pumpkin feels out of place but also as if it has always been there – quietly part of the landscape, despite its odd appearance.

Naoshima has become one of Japan's most distinctive art destinations. Under the vision of Benesse Art Site Naoshima – a project that combines art, architecture and nature – the island hosts more than 10 museums, installations and site-specific works spread across beaches, forests and fishing villages. Kusama's *Pumpkin* is one of its most recognisable landmarks and a key symbol of the island's unique approach to placing art in the everyday landscape.

The sculpture was installed in 1994 and was Kusama's first permanent outdoor work on Naoshima. Made from fibreglass-reinforced plastic, it is about two metres tall and two and a half metres wide. The dots are a constant in Kusama's work. She began using them after childhood hallucinations in which her world seemed covered in small, repeated patterns. On the pumpkin, the dots multiply over and over, spreading across the surface without clear beginning or end. The choice of a pumpkin – a simple vegetable – adds to the work's complexity. It is familiar, even ordinary, but here it becomes something to look at and think about.

In 2021, a typhoon knocked the sculpture into the sea. It was later recovered and rebuilt with a stronger exterior. That event added a new layer to the work: a reminder that even the most solid things can be vulnerable.

ABOUT YAYOI KUSAMA

Yayoi Kusama was born in 1929 in Matsumoto, Japan. She is known for her immersive installations, bold use of polka dots, and repeated motifs. Her work spans painting, sculpture, performance and large-scale installations. Themes of infinity, obsession and self-obliteration run throughout her practice, often rooted in hallucinations she experienced as a child. Pumpkins, nets and mirrored spaces are recurring visual elements in her work.

'Our earth is only one polka dot among a million stars in the cosmos. Polka dots are a way to infinity. When we obliterate nature and our bodies with polka dots, we become part of the unity of our environment.'

Yayoi Kusama

Three must-see artworks at Benesse Art Site Naoshima

- **WALTER DE MARIA, Time/Timeless/No Time**
  In the Chichu Art Museum you will find Walter De Maria's *Time/Timeless/No Time*. A huge granite sphere stands in a bright room, surrounded by wooden beams covered in gold leaf. As the daylight shifts, the room changes too, making the artwork look different every time you see it. De Maria designed the work especially for Naoshima, making it one of only a few permanent installations by the artist (p. 174) in Asia.

- **GEORGE RICKEY, Three Squares Vertical Diagonal**
  Outside Benesse House, you will come across George Rickey's moving sculpture *Three Squares Vertical Diagonal*. Three shiny metal squares are fixed to long arms and slowly turn in the wind. Depending on the weather, the movement may be gentle or fast, almost like a dance. Rickey was a pioneer of kinetic art. His carefully engineered works are surprisingly sensitive to even the slightest breeze.

- **YAYOI KUSAMA, Red Pumpkin**
  At Miyanoura Port, Yayoi Kusama's *Red Pumpkin* is impossible to miss. Covered in bold black dots, this bright red sculpture is hollow, and you can even step inside. It is the very first artwork that many visitors see when they arrive on Naoshima.

George Rickey, Three Squares Vertical Diagonal

Benesse Art Site Naoshima

Africa

38.

Hassan Darsi

Jetée en or

Al Maaden Sculpture Park, Marrakech, Morocco

At Al Maaden Sculpture Park, set on a golf course near Marrakech, Hassan Darsi's *Jetée en or (Golden pier)* appears like a scattered line of large geometric shapes. The work consists of multiple golden cubes resting directly on the ground. Each one catches the sunlight, casting bright reflections across the grass. They're arranged in what seems like a random pattern, as if in motion. But their careful placement is deliberate, creating an organised composition that spreads light throughout the area.

During the day, the installation plays with light and shadow: each cube shines brightly, creating a path marked by flashes of gold and soft shadows. At dusk, the work transforms again. A lighting system illuminates the cubes, marking their line like a beacon or the beam of a lighthouse, connecting the piece to the changing light of day and night. The cubes shift from cool, metallic reflections by day to a warm, glowing appearance at night.

By coating these simple forms in his signature gold adhesive – a material inspired by decorative finishes in Casablanca – Darsi turns ordinary blocks into striking, reflective sculptures. The shiny gold surfaces attract attention and suggest luxury, but they also carry a more critical message. Gold is a symbol of wealth and status that also reminds viewers how these things are unequally shared. The cubes in a way resemble small shipping containers or vaults, hinting at global trade, migration and the unequal value placed on goods, people and cultures.

ABOUT HASSAN DARSI

Hassan Darsi was born in 1961 in Casablanca, Morocco. He is known for his thoughtful, site-specific works that explore themes of urban transformation, power and social inequality. He often uses gilding and reflective materials to question notions of value and beauty. His projects, which range from public interventions to sculptural installations, invite viewers to rethink space, ownership and heritage. By working with architectural forms, urban planning and symbolic materials like gold leaf, Darsi critiques both local and global power structures.

Museum of African Contemporary Art Al Maaden

Three other art stops in Marrakech

- **MUSEUM OF AFRICAN CONTEMPORARY ART AL MAADEN**
  The Museum of African Contemporary Art Al Maaden (MACAAL) is located adjacent to the Al Maaden Sculpture Park. The collection is dedicated exclusively to contemporary African art and consists of works by various prominent Moroccan artists.

- **GALLERY WALK**
  Marrakech has a small but vibrant contemporary gallery scene, perfect for an afternoon stroll to discover the latest developments within the city's contemporary artworld. Start your art walk at Comptoir des Mines Galerie, a Marrakech art world staple.

- **JARDIN MAJORELLE AND MUSÉE YVES SAINT LAURENT**
  Fashion designer Yves Saint Laurent saved the famous Jardin Majorelle, created in the 1920s and '30s by French painter Jacques Majorelle. He conceived a striking cobalt pigment – later known as Majorelle Blue – and splashed it across walls, fountains and pavilions. The colour is meant to resemble the Moroccan sky and the colours of the region's tiles. The Musée Yves Saint Laurent Marrakech sits just steps from the beautiful gardens and is housed in a striking terracotta-brick building. Inside, it showcases around 1,000 couture garments, accessories, sketches and photographs, organised thematically to reflect YSL's inspirations: Africa, Morocco, gardens and art.

Marrakech

Jardin Majorelle and Musée Yves Saint Laurent

39.

Tiago Rodrigues
The Sound of My Voice

Spier Art Collection, Stellenbosch, South Africa

The Sound of My Voice is an installation on Spier Wine Farm in Stellenbosch. It consists of tall, narrow, precisely carved lettering that spells out the phrase 'soon it will be quiet', standing upright before the historic slave bell on the farm. It stands as a contemporary reckoning with a layered, painful past.

Founded in 1692, Spier was among the first colonial farms in Stellenbosch. But before its establishment – and the annexation of this land by European settlers – it was inhabited and cultivated for centuries by Indigenous Khoekhoe and San communities with rich farming and pastoral traditions. These histories were violently disrupted by dispossession, forced labour and slavery, which established systems of racial hierarchy that would shape South Africa for generations.

One of the most visible signifiers of this colonial legacy is the Spier Slave Bell, built in 1825, and once used to regiment and control the lives of enslaved people forced to work on the lands. Today, the bell remains on Spier's grounds as a historical artefact. While it represents an important act of preservation and a commendable acknowledgement of the past, one might also consider whether highlighting this history through the art collection could be complemented by more visible references to this history elsewhere on the estate to deepen the conversation.

Rodrigues's *The Sound of My Voice* is inspired by Brett Bailey's fictional enslaved character Sannie de Goede, who says on the eve of emancipation, 'Ring your bell, meneer. Ring it loud, for soon it will be quiet'. By using the last part of this quote for his work, the artist confronts the bell's historic function and personifies its voice, suggesting that the master's authority will one day be silenced, while acknowledging its lingering echoes.

ABOUT TIAGO RODRIGUES

Tiago Rodrigues was born in 1988 in Cape Town, South Africa. His work explores transgression and breaking barriers: through repetitive, labour-intensive processes and the use of text, he transforms symbols of violence into formal beauty. Balancing poetry and provocation, his sculptures and installations invite critical reflection on power and history, encouraging us to see the world in more honest and inclusive ways.

Zeitz MOCAA

Three tips for art in Cape Town

- **ZEITZ MOCAA**
  The Zeitz Museum of Contemporary Art Africa (Zeitz MOCAA) is housed in a transformed historic grain silo at Cape Town's V&A Waterfront and features dramatic cathedral-like interiors. As the largest museum of contemporary African art, it showcases diverse, cutting-edge works from across the continent.

- **CAPE TOWN'S GALLERY SCENE**
  Exploring Cape Town's vibrant gallery scene is a must for any art lover. At Stevenson gallery, for instance, you will find contemporary art that tackles social and political issues with strong local and international relevance. Across the street at blank projects gallery, you encounter experimental, conceptual work from emerging African artists exploring new ideas and forms.

- **BO-KAAP**
  The Bo-Kaap neighbourhood offers a glimpse into Cape Town's rich Cape Malay heritage and is also worth visiting for its vividly painted houses, cobbled streets and stunning views of Table Mountain.

Bo-Kaap

Spier Wine Farm

40.

Yinka Shonibare
Wind Sculpture (SG) III

The Norval Foundation, Cape Town, South Africa

Wind Sculpture (SG) III is a monumental outdoor work in the Norval Foundation's Sculpture Garden, just south of Cape Town. Towering seven metres high, two and a half metres wide and two metres deep, the sculpture is composed of a steel armature supporting a hand-painted fibreglass cast.

The sculpture is part of Yinka Shonibare's ongoing *Wind Sculpture* series, which seeks to make the invisible visible: capturing the fluid, dynamic motion of fabric caught in the wind and rendering it permanently in solid form. The result is a striking, gravity-defying structure that seems to billow and twist, frozen in time.

What immediately stands out is the use of bold, vibrant colours, meticulously painted to resemble Dutch wax, or batik fabric. These textiles, often thought of as quintessentially West African, have a layered history: they are originally inspired by Indonesian batik, industrially produced in the Netherlands and embraced in African markets. By referencing these patterns, Shonibare exposes the entangled histories of colonial trade, migration and cultural exchange. The vibrant designs are not mere decoration but a statement about the hybridity of identity itself – how culture is never static, but shaped by movement, adaptation, appropriation and power dynamics.

Set among the indigenous plants of the Norval Foundation's Sculpture Garden, *Wind Sculpture (SG) III*'s vivid colours blaze against the landscape. It becomes both landmark and provocation – inviting viewers to consider how the unseen 'winds' of history, commerce and migration continue to shape who we are, both individually and collectively.

ABOUT YINKA SHONIBARE

Yinka Shonibare was born in 1962 in London, UK. The British–Nigerian artist is renowned for exploring colonialism, cultural identity and globalisation. Best known for his use of brightly coloured Dutch wax fabrics – symbolic of complex trade histories – he reimagines European art and history through a sharp postcolonial lens.

Nandipha Mntambo, Ophelia

Other highlights of the Norval Foundation's Sculpture Garden

- **WILLIAM KENTRIDGE, Action**
  William Kentridge is one of South Africa's most renowned artists, whose work is exhibited in museums, galleries and public spaces around the world. Best known for his video art, he often returns to the medium of film as a central theme in his practice. At the Norval Foundation, his monumental bronze sculpture *Action* depicts a vintage film camera – a direct homage to this beloved medium.

- **NANDIPHA MNTAMBO, Ophelia**
  In the pond of the Norval Foundation's Sculpture Garden lies Nandipha Mntambo's half-submerged artwork *Ophelia*. Crafted from steel, the sculpture depicts Ophelia – a tragic character from Shakespeare's *Hamlet* – resting among aquatic plants. In the play, Ophelia descends into madness, which ultimately leads to her drowning. Mntambo's sculpture captures this haunting moment, merging the natural setting with themes of vulnerability, tragedy, loss and decay.

- **EDOARDO VILLA, Africa**
  Edoarda Villa was an Italian-born South African sculptor whose abstract steel and bronze works explore the human figure through bold, geometric forms. Villa's large steel sculpture *Africa* blends Cubist abstraction with references to traditional African masks and figurative forms.

William Kentridge, Action

NORVAL FOUNDATION
GRUB

The Norval Foundation

Credits

Images — Cover image: Installation view, Ugo Rondinone, *Seven Magic Mountains*, 2016-present. Photo Yan - stock.adobe.com — **7, 9, 10-11, 12**: Wikimedia Commons — **15**: © Saffron Pape — **18**: Alicja Kwade, Installation view of *Pars pro Toto*, 2018. Louisiana Museum of Modern Art, Humlebaek, Denmark. Acquired with fundings from Museumsfonden af 7. december 1966, donations from louisiana.dk and fundings from sale of Louisiana Editions. © Alicja Kwade. Courtesy of the artist and KÖNIG GALERIE, Berlin. Photo © Louisiana Museum of Modern Art, Humlebaek, Denmark / Kim Hansen — **21**: Alexander Farnsworth, iStock — **22-23**: Anselm Kiefer, *Die Himmelspaläste*, 2003-2018. © Anselm Kiefer. Photo © Charles Duprat Courtesy of Eschaton – Anselm Kiefer Foundation — **24-25**: Anselm Kiefer, *Die Frauen der Antike* – Ensemble of 17 sculptures, 1999-2002. © Anselm Kiefer. Photo © Charles Duprat. Courtesy of Eschaton – Anselm Kiefer Foundation — **26**: Anselm Kiefer, *Zu den Müttern – Steigend, steigend sinke nieder*, 2016. © Anselm Kiefer. Photo © Georges Poncet. Courtesy of Eschaton – Anselm Kiefer Foundation — **27**: Parc des Ateliers, LUMA Arles, France. © Adrian Deweerdt — **28**: Daniel Buren, Photo-souvenir: *Sulle vigne: punti di vista*, permanent work in situ, Castello di Ama, 2001. Detail © DB - SABAM Belgium 2026. Photo © Alessandro Moggi, courtesy Collezione Castello di Ama — **31**: courtesy Collezione Castello di Ama — **32-33, 34-35, 36**: Grayson Perry, *A House for Essex*, 2015. Photo © Jack Hobhouse. Courtesy of Living Architecture UK — **37**: Atelier Van Lieshout, *CasAnus*, 2007. Photo © Tineke Schuurmans. Courtesy of Verbeke Foundation — **38-39**: James Lee Byars, *The Spinning Oracle of Delphi*, 1986. ©The Estate of James Lee Byars, courtesy Galerie Michael Werner Berlin Märkisch Wilmersdorf, London, Köln und New York, and Museum Schloss Moyland. Photo © Stiftung Museum Schloss Moyland/Florian Monheim and Roman von Götz — **40:** © JoopS, iStock — **41**: Courtesy Castello di Rivoli Museo d'Arte Contemporanea, Rivoli-Torino. Photo © Andrea Guermani. Courtesy of Castello di Rivoli — **42-43**: Art & Language, *A BAD PLACE*. Photo © LinkxTV. Courtesy of Château de Montsoreau – Museum of Contemporary Art — **44, 46**: Jeff Koons, *Apollo Wind Spinner*, 2020-2022. © Jeff Koons. Photos © Eftychia Vlachou, courtesy of the DESTE Foundation for Contemporary Art — **47**: © Rubén G. Perdomo, Courtesy of Fundació Pilar I Joan Miró a Mallorca — **48**: Jenny Holzer, *Untitled*, 1991, carving on rock, Truisms, 1977–79. Permanent installation: Furka Pass, Switzerland. © Jenny Holzer, member Artists Rights Society (ARS), New York / © SABAM Belgium 2026. Photo © Claude Joray. Courtesy the artist and Hauser & Wirth — **50**: Josette Taramarcaz, *Arche*, 2011. Photo © Josette Taramarcaz, courtesy of The Verbier 3-D Foundation — **51**: Rana Begum, *No. 1387 Fence*, 2024. Photo © Melody Sky, courtesy of The Verbier 3-D Foundation — **52**: Jeppe Hein, *Path of Emotions*, 2018. Collection Carmignac. © Jeppe Hein. Photo © Thibaut Chapotot for the Fondation Carmignac. Courtesy of Fondation Carmignac — **54**: NILS-UDO, *La Couvée*, 2018. Collection Carmignac. © NILS-UDO | Photo © NILS-UDO. Courtesy of NILS-UDO and Fondation Carmignac — **55**: Adrián Villar Rojas, *The most beautiful of all mothers (XII)*, 2015. Collection Carmignac, courtesy the artist and Marian Goodman Gallery. Photo © Camille Moirenc for the Fondation Carmignac. Courtesy of Fondation Carmignac — **56-57**: Laure Prouvost, *Touching to Sea you through our Extremities*, 2021. © Triennial Beaufort - Westtoer apb / © SABAM Belgium 2026. Courtesy of Triennial Beaufort — **59**: View of Karnak at Kanaal with terracotta spheres by Bosco Sodi. © Bosco Sodi and Axel Vervoordt Gallery — **60**: Marc Quinn, *All Of Nature Flows Through Us*, 2011. Courtesy of Kistefos Museum, Norway. Photo © Einar Aslaksen — **62**: Yayoi Kusama, *Shine of Life*, 2019. Kistefos. © YAYOI KUSAMA. Courtesy Ota Fine Arts and Victoria Miro. Photo © Einar Aslaksen. Courtesy of Kistefos Museum, Norway

— **63, 64-65**: The Twist, Kistefos Museum © Wirestock, iStock — **66-67**: Martin Creed, *Work No. 2792*, 2017. Collection museum Voorlinden. © SABAM Belgium 2026. Courtesy of museum Voorlinden — **68**: Garden of Piet Oudolf at Voorlinden © Eric van Lokven — **69**: Tracey Emin, *I want My Time With You*, 2017. © Tracey Emin. All rights reserved, SABAM Belgium 2026. Photo © Alena Kravchenko, iStock — **70**: Martin Puryear, *Meditation in a Beech Wood*, 1996. © Martin Puryear, courtesy Matthew Marks Gallery. Photo © Robert Damisch, courtesy of the artist and Wanås Konst — **72**: Martin Puryear, *Meditation in a Beech Wood*, 1996. © Martin Puryear, courtesy Matthew Marks Gallery. Photo © Anders Norrsell, courtesy of the artist and Wanås Konst — **73**: Robert Wilson, *A House for Edwin Denby*, 2000. Photo © Anders Norrsell, courtesy of the artist and Wanås Konst — **74-75**: Aerial view of Wanås Estate with the sculpture park and Wanås Castle. Photo © Per Pixel, courtesy of Wanås Konst — **76-77**: Niki de Saint Phalle, *Il Giardino dei Tarocchi (The Tarot Garden)*, 1979-1998. © 2026 Fondazione Il Giardino dei Tarocchi / SABAM Belgium. Photo © starmaro, iStock — **78:** Niki de Saint Phalle, *Fontaine aux Nanas,* 1991. © 2026 Fondazione Il Giardino dei Tarocchi / SABAM Belgium. Photo © starmaro, iStock — **80**: Olafur Eliasson, *Our glacial perspective*, 2020. Installation view: Hochjochferner glacier, South Tyrol. © 2020 Olafur Eliasson. Commissioned by Talking Waters Society. Photo © Oskar Da Riz. Courtesy of studio Olafur Eliasson — **82-83, 84**: Olafur Eliasson, *Our glacial perspective*, 2020. Installation view: Hochjochferner glacier, South Tyrol. © 2020 Olafur Eliasson. Commissioned by Talking Waters Society. Photo © Oskar Da Riz. Courtesy of studio Olafur Eliasson — **86-87**: Oudolf Field. Hauser & Wirth Somerset. Photo © Jason Ingram. Courtesy of Hauser & Wirth — **88-89**: Radić Pavilion, designed by Smiljan Radić, 2014. Hauser & Wirth Somerset. Photo © Jason Ingram. Courtesy of Hauser & Wirth — **90**: Oudolf Field. Hauser & Wirth Somerset. Photo © Jason Ingram. Courtesy of Hauser & Wirth — **91**: © georgeclerck, iStock — **92-93**: Pipilotti Rist, *Nordic Pixel Forest*, 2024. © courtesy of the Artist, Hauser & Wirth and Luhring Augustine / BONO / © SABAM Belgium 2026. Photo © Kristina Aurore Kvåle / Ekebergparken. Courtesy of Ekebergparken — **95**: Wikimedia Commons — **96-97**: © Fujiko Nakaya, *Pathfinder #18700*, 2018. © Fujiko Nakaya / BONO. Photo © Kristina Aurore Kvåle / Ekebergparken. Courtesy of Ekebergparken — **98**: Sophie Calle, *Dead End*, 2018. Courtesy of the artist, Perrotin and Château La Coste. © SABAM Belgium 2026. Photo © Nienke van der Wal — **101**: © Paul Matisse, *Meditation Bell*, 2012. Courtesy of Château La Coste — **102-103**: © Richard Haughton. Courtesy of Château La Coste — **104**: Tracey Emin, *I Lay Here For You*, 2018. © Tracey Emin. All rights reserved, SABAM Belgium 2026. Courtesy of Jupiter Artland. Photo © Allan Pollok Morris – Photography — **107**: © Guven Ozdemir, iStock — **108**: Yoko Ono, *IMAGINE PEACE TOWER*, 2007. Viðey Island, Reykjavík, Iceland. © Yoko Ono. Photo by TetsuRo Hamada © Yoko Ono — **110**: Yoko Ono, *Wish Tree*, 2019. © Yoko Ono. Photo © Nienke van der Wal — **111**: Yoko Ono, *Play It By Trust*, 1966/1999. © Yoko Ono. Collection of the artist, on permanent loan to LongHouse. Photo © Philippe Cheng. Courtesy of LongHouse — **112, 114-115**: Zhang Enli, *A Cheerful Person*, 2021. Church of San Rocco, Montabone. Photo © Giorgio Perottino/ Artissima. Courtesy of the artist and Hauser & Wirth — **117**: © Ladiras, iStock — **120**: Ai Weiwei, *Iron Tree*, 2013. © Ai Weiwei Studio; courtesy of Ai Weiwei Studio and Frederik Meijer Gardens & Sculpture Park — **122**: Ai Weiwei, *Iron Tree*, 2013. © Ai Weiwei Studio; courtesy of Ai Weiwei Studio, Lisson Gallery and Frederik Meijer Gardens & Sculpture Park. Photo © Dean VanDis — **123**: Zhang Huan, *Long Island Buddha*, 2010-2011. © Zhang Huan Studio, courtesy of Pace Gallery and Frederik Meijer Gardens & Sculpture Park and Pace Gallery — **124**: Elmgreen & Dragset,

Prada Marfa. 2005. © Elmgreen & Dragset / SABAM Belgium 2026. Courtesy: Art Production Fund, New York; Ballroom Marfa, Marfa; the artists. Photo © James Evans — **127**: © Lone Star Stock, iStock — **128-129**: Hélio Oiticica, *Invenção da cor, Penetrável Magic Square #5, De Luxe*, 1978. Photo © Tati Campelo, iStock — **130-131**: © AlexandreFagundes, iStock — **133**: Olafur Eliasson, *Viewing machine*, 2001/2008. Installation view: Inhotim Centro de Arte Contemporânea, Brumadinho, Minas Gerais, Brazil, 2010. © 2001/2008 Olafur Eliasson. Courtesy of the artist; Inhotim Centro de Arte Contemporânea, Brazil. Photo © Jochen Volz. Courtesy of studio Olafur Eliasson — **134-135**: Yayoi Kusama, *Narcissus Garden*, 2009. ©YAYOI KUSAMA. Courtesy of Ota Fine Arts and David Zwirner. — **136**: Hugh Hayden, *Huff and a Puff*, 2023. © Hugh Hayden. deCordova Sculpture Park and Museum, The Trustees. Lead support for Art at The Trustees provided by Mr. Richard M. Coffman and Mrs. Gabrielle C.F. Coffman. Additional support provided by Lisson Gallery, the National Endowment for the Arts, and the Next Generation Fund of the Roy A. Hunt Foundation, 2023.6. Photo: Mel Taing — **138**: deCordova Sculpture Park and Museum, The Trustees, Lincoln, Massachusetts, courtesy of Above Summit — **140-141**: Do Ho Suh, *Fallen Star*, 2012. Steel-frame house, concrete foundation, brick, chimney, garden, lawn chairs, table, hibachi-style grill, bird bath and bird house. Approx. 457.2 × 548.6 cm. Photography by Erik Jepsen, UCSD, Stuart Collection. Courtesy the artist and Stuart Collection, University of California San Diego, CA, USA. © Do Ho Suh. Courtesy the artist and Lehmann Maupin, New York, Seoul, and London — **142:** © pinglabel, iStock — **144**: Bodega Colomé — **145**: © R.M. Nunes, Shutterstock — **146-147**: Maya Lin, *Storm King Wavefield*, 2007-2008. Storm King Art Center, Mountainville, NY. © Maya Lin Studio, courtesy Pace Gallery. Photo © Jerry L. Thompson — **149**: Alicja Kwade, *LinienLand*, 2018. Storm King Art Center, Mountainville, NY. © Alicja Kwade, courtesy Pace Gallery. Photo © Jeffrey Jenkins — **150-151**: Pascale Marthine Tayou, *Mikado Tree*, 2010, at the Donum Estate. The Donum Collection®. © SABAM Belgium 2026. Courtesy of The Donum Collection. Photo © Robert Berg — **152**: Yayoi Kusama, *Pumpkin*, 2014. ©YAYOI KUSAMA. Courtesy of The Donum Collection. Courtesy of Ota Fine Arts. Photo © Robert Berg — **154-155**: Zhan Wang, *Artificial Rock No. 126*, 2007-2013. © Zhan Wang, courtesy Matthew Marks Gallery Courtesy and The Donum Collection. Photo © Robert Berg — 156: Simone Leigh, *Satellite*, 2022. © Simone Leigh, courtesy Matthew Marks Gallery — **158**: Felix Gonzalez-Torres, *"Untitled"*, 1992-1995. Installed at Glenstone, Potomac, MD. 12 Mar. 2008-ongoing. © Estate Felix Gonzalez-Torres, courtesy of the Felix Gonzalez-Torres Foundation and Glenstone Museum. Photo © Jerry Thompson — **159**: Robert Gober, *Two Partially Buried Sinks*, 1986-1987. Installed at Glenstone, Potomac, MD. © Robert Gober, courtesy Matthew Marks Gallery and Glenstone Museum — **160-161**: Jeff Koons, *Split-Rocker*, 2000. © Jeff Koons. Courtesy of Studio Jeff Koons and Glenstone Museum — **162, 164-165**: Susan Philipsz, *We'll All Go Together*, 2009. Powder Mountain, Eden, Utah. Courtesy the artist and Tanya Bonakdar Gallery, New York. Photo © Drew Rane — **167**: Gerard & Kelly, *Relay (Powder Mountain)*, 2024. Powder Mountain, Eden, Utah. © SABAM Belgium 2026. Photo © Drew Rane. Courtesy of the artists — **168-169**: Griffin Loop, *Launch Intention*, 2014. Powder Mountain, Eden, Utah. Courtesy of the artist — **170-171, 172**: Installation view, Ugo Rondinone, *Seven Magic Mountains*, 2016 - present. Photos courtesy of the Nevada Museum of Art — **176**: Walter De Maria, *The Lightning Field*, 1977. Long-term installation, western New Mexico.© Estate of Walter De Maria. Photo © John Cliett, courtesy Dia Art Foundation, New York — **177**: Walter De Maria, *The Broken Kilometer*, 1979. © The Estate of Walter De Maria. Photo © Jon Abbott, courtesy Dia Art Foundation, New York — **180-181, 182-183**: Antony Gormley, *Inside Australia*, 2003. Commission for 50th Perth International Arts Festival. Permanent installation, Lake Ballard, Menzies, Western

Australia. Photo © Frances Andrijich and the artist — **184**: Antony Gormley, *Exposure*, 2010. Photo © Nienke van der Wal and the artist — **186**: Daniel Libeskind. *Outside Line*, Uozu, Japan. 1997. Courtesy studio Libeskind / Twaki — **188**: Ryoji Ikeda, *spectra*, 2018. Collection Mona (Museum of Old and New Art). Photo © Mona/Jesse Hunniford, image courtesy Mona (Museum of Old and New Art), Hobart, Tasmania, Australia — **190-191**: Ryoji Ikeda, *spectra*, 2018. Collection Museum of Old and New Art (Mona). Photo © Mona/Jacob Collings, image courtesy Museum of Old and New Art (Mona), Hobart, Tasmania, Australia — **192-193**: Fujiko Nakaya, *Khao Yai Fog Forest, Fog Landscape #48435*, 2024. © Fujiko Nakaya. Khao Yai Art Forest, courtesy Khao Yai Art. Photo © Andrea Rossetti — **195**: Araya Rasdjarmrearnsook, *Two Planets Series*, 2008. Khao Yai Art Forest, courtesy Khao Yai Art. Photo © Krittawat Atthsis and Puttisin Choojesroom — **196-197**: ubatsat, *Pilgrimage to Eternity*, 2024. Khao Yai Art Forest, courtesy Khao Yai Art. Photo © Andrea Rossetti — **198-199**: Louise Bourgeois, *Maman*, 1999. Installed in the outdoor garden of Ho-Am Art Museum, Gyeonggi-do, South Korea, 2023. Photo © Ho-am Art Museum. © The Easton Foundation/VAGA at ARS, New York and SABAM Belgium 2026. — **201**: © LouisHiemstra, iStock — **202-203**: © Pierrick Lemaret, iStock — **204-205**: Richard Serra, *East-West/ West-East*, 2014. © SABAM Belgium 2026. Photo © Davor Flam, Shutterstock — **206**: © sonmez, iStock — **207**: Monira Al Qadiri, *Zephyr*, 2022. Commissioned by Qatar Museums. Photo © Sarjoun Faour. Courtesy of the artist — **208-209**: Yayoi Kusama, *Pumpkin*, 2022. ©YAYOI KUSAMA. Photo © Tadasu Yamamoto. Courtesy of Benesse Art Site Naoshima — **211**: George Rickey, *Three Squares Vertical Diagonal*, 1972-1982. © George Rickey Estate, LLC / SABAM Belgium 2026. Photo © Maritxu, Shutterstock — **212-213**: Benesse Art Site Naoshima — **216-217**: Hassan Darsi, *Jetée en or*, 2011. Parc de sculpture Al Maaden. © SABAM Belgium 2026. Courtesy of the artist — **218**: © Ayoub El Bardii — **219**: © margouillatphotos, iStock — **220-221**: © Balate Dorin, iStock — **222-223**: Tiago Rodrigues, *The Sound of My Voice*, 2019. Courtesy of Spier Art Collection — **224**: © Murmakova, iStock — **225**: © Boogich, iStock — **226-227**: © Spier Wine Farm — **228**: Yinka Shonibare, *Wind Sculpture (SG) III*, 2018. Courtesy of Norval Foundation. © SABAM Belgium 2026. Photo © Dave Southwood — **230**: Nandipha Mntambo, *Ophelia*, 2015. Courtesy of Norval Foundation — **231**: William Kentridge, *Action (Large Glyph)*, 2019. © William Kentridge. Courtesy of Norval Foundation — **232-233**: William Kentridge, *Processione di Riparazioniste 10*, 2017. © William Kentridge. Photo © Wieland Gleich. Courtesy of Norval Foundation

Quotes — **20**: 303gallery.com/news/alicja-kwade-hypothetical-reality — **30**: lampoonmagazine.com/daniel-buren-interview-painter-contemporary-art-paintings-vertical-stripes-fabric-glass-wood-flags — **58**: musee-lam.fr/en/laure-prouvost — **79**: guggenheim-bilbao.eus/en/exhibition/pintarla-violencia — **94**: artforum.com/columns/pipilotti-rist-speaks-about-her-exhibition-at-the-new-museum-231244 — **100**: interviewmagazine.com/art/sophie-calle — **106**: myartbroker.com/artist-tracey-emin/articles/tracey-emin-autobiography-femininity-modern-art — **126**: Inger Christensen, It, 1969 — **132**: spectator.co.uk/article/true-colours — **148:** arts.gov/stories/blog/2018/tuesdaythought-maya-lin — **166**: goodwoodartfoundation.org/art/artists/susan-philipsz — **194**: theglasshouse.org/whats-on/fujiko-nakaya-veil — **200**: newyorker.com magazine/2002/02/04/the-spiders-web — **210**: guggenheim-bilbao.eus/en exhibition/biocosmic

Acknowledgements

We are deeply grateful to all the artists, photographers, institutions, galleries and estates that contributed to this book. Without your help and generosity, this book would not have been possible. We are thankful that you believe in our mission to share these works with the world – even if only on paper.

We are in awe of every single one of the artists that we featured in this book. It has been a true pleasure to dive head first into their spectacular works and look for the stories behind each one. We recognise how demanding it is to be an artist and how much dedication and persistence are required to bring these large-scale projects to life. This effort deserves even more appreciation today, at a time when the urgency and relevance of art are too often questioned or undervalued.

We also want to express our appreciation for the institutions dedicated to preserving these works. The fact that these works are all exposed to the elements means caring for them is no easy task. We hope your efforts will ensure that these artworks remain safe for future generations to enjoy.

We are very grateful for the support and guidance of our publisher Lannoo, and specifically Carolijn Domensino and Eline Maeyens. Thank you for believing in this project, even when at times it seemed impossible to pull off. But we did it! And we have you to thank for it. We also want to extend our deepest gratitude to Han van de Ven, who made this book come to life with his fantastic design, and to Julia Grandison, for her thoughtful and meticulous treatment of our book.

We want to thank our amazing team: Flor Linckens, Kika de Rooij and Barbara Boschman. Not only is it a true pleasure to work with people who are the very best at what they do, it is even better when they are as passionate about art and travel as you are. Thank you for helping us bring this book into the world.

We want to thank everyone who contributed to making this book a reality through our crowdfunding, and particularly Marco van Thiel and Maarten Groeneveld. Your trust in us means everything!

We would also like to thank our loved ones: Ahmet, Mila and Rik. However, it is, in this case, debatable whether they should perhaps be thanking us for taking them to so many breathtaking destinations in the name of research. All joking aside, we are enormously grateful to have the best travel companions and most supportive families. Making a book is fun on paper, but in reality, means many late nights and lost weekends. Thank you for your loving support!

And last but not least: thank you, dear reader, for picking up this book. We hope you love it as much as we loved making it.

Nadine van den Bosch
Nienke van der Wal

THE ART *TRAVEL* BOOK

40 iconic outdoor artworks

Concept / Text
Nadine van den Bosch
Nienke van der Wal

Book Design
Han van de Ven

Copy Editing
Julia Grandison

Sign up for our newsletter with news about new and forthcoming publications on art, interior design, travel, photography and fashion as well as exclusive offers and events. If you have any questions or comments about the material in this book, please do not hesitate to contact our editorial team: art@lannoo.com

BISAC: ART062000, TRV016000
D/2026/45/2
ISBN: 978-90-599-6050-3
www.lannoopublishers.com